BÉT

W9-BKY-851

History—remembered, recovered, invented

YESHIVA UNIVERSITY

*The Benjamin Gottesman Lectures have been established
at Yeshiva University by his family on the occasion
of his seventieth birthday and in recognition of
his long interest in Yeshiva University of which he
has been a trustee since 1927.*

*For the Gottesman Lectures, Yeshiva University invites
people of outstanding achievement to deliver
lectures of scholarly and creative significance.
Lecturers are encouraged to broaden the focus of
academic inquiry and to explore implications
in their scholarship for larger intellectual
and social problems.*

HISTORY

Remembered, Recovered, Invented

Bernard Lewis

Princeton University Press

Princeton, New Jersey

Wingate College Library

Copyright © 1975 by Princeton University Press

All Rights Reserved

Library of Congress Cataloging in Publication Data will
be found on the last printed page of this book

This book has been composed in Linotype Janson and Granjon

Printed in the United States of America
by Princeton University Press,
Princeton, New Jersey

For P.

so much, so little

064217

09131.

Preface

From time to time the historian needs to leave his period, his area, and his topic, and take a broader look at the nature of his vocation and discipline. This is what I have tried to do in these pages. While my illustrative examples are naturally chosen in the main from the Middle Eastern history with which I am most familiar, I have tried to achieve some deeper insights and reach some more general conclusions about the nature of historical knowledge, study, and writing, and about their functions and purposes in human societies.

The occasion to formulate these reflections was provided by an invitation to deliver the Gottesman lectures for 1974 at Yeshiva University in New York City, and I should like to express my thanks both to the university and to its generous benefactor for making this possible. A word of appreciation is also due to my attentive and alert audiences at Yeshiva University, whose comments and questions enabled me to remove several blemishes from my original text.

Finally, I should like to thank my friends Professors Elie Kedourie and Michael Zand for help and advice on some of the matters discussed in these lectures.

B.L.

Contents

History—remembered, recovered, invented

.

CHAPTER ONE

MASADA AND CYRUS

The celebration of historical events by commemorative festivals is an ancient Middle Eastern custom which still survives. In modern times such commemorations are state occasions; in earlier days they were usually religious feasts and fasts. In recent years the new and independent states of the Middle East and elsewhere have added many new historical anniversaries, commemorating successive revolutions and liberations, as coup follows coup, each presented as a "national day." More recently some important medieval events have been remembered and celebrated. Notable among them are the Turkish conquest of Constantinople, the 500th anniversary of which was honored in Turkey in 1953, the festivities in Cairo in 1969 for the 1,000th anniversary of the foundation of the city by the Fatimid caliph al-Muʿizz, and the celebration by the Turks in 1971 of the 900th anniversary of the decisive battle of Manzikert, which decided that Anatolia was to be a Turkish-Muslim land and no longer a Greek and Christian land. Besides these, there are public and private, local and national, celebrations of the births and deaths of various sages and heroes, many of whom enjoy several birthplaces and several nationalities. In the words of Thomas Heywood,

> Seven cities warred for Homer, being dead,
> Who, living, had no roof to shroud his head.

The 1,000th anniversary of the birth of Avicenna (by the Muslim calendar) was celebrated by Arabs, Persians, and Turks, each claiming him as a compatriot. His birthplace, near Bukhara, even earned him posthumous annexation as a culture hero of the Soviet Union, through his retrospective citizenship of the Soviet Socialist Federal Republic of Uzbekistan.

Commemorations based on ancient history, where memories are faint and dates uncertain, are less frequent, but there have been two such celebrations in the Middle East in recent years, both of which became major events in their respective countries. One was the commemoration of the heroic defense and final fall of Masada in the Jewish revolt against the Romans in A.D. 66. The other was the celebration in Iran, under the auspices of the Shah himself, of the 2,500 anniversary of the foundation of the Persian state and monarchy by Cyrus the Great.

The two have many features in common. Both are primarily political and military and not, like earlier commemorations based on antiquity, religious. Both enjoyed a large measure of state sponsorship. The Cyrus commemoration was due directly to the initiative of the Shah. The Masada commemoration, if not initiated, was adopted by the Israeli state and made the center of something verging on a national cult. Expressions of this were the solemn reinterment in a military cemetery, with full honors, of the bones found in the ruins of Masada, and the adoption of the practice of swearing in the Israeli paratroops on the ruins of Masada, with the formula "Masada shall not fall again."[1] Both have been made the foci of great national festivities. Though the one commemorates a victory and the founding of a state, the other a defeat and the destruction of a state, both share the common theme of dedication and heroism interpreted in a national sense.

Both themes—Masada and Cyrus—also share another feature: that they had been forgotten and were unknown among their own peoples, and were recovered from outside sources. The Rabbinic and other Jewish tradition knows nothing of Masada. The name is not mentioned in the rich Rabbinic literature; even the Hebrew spelling of the name is conjectural. The sole source from which we derive our information on the heroic deaths of the defenders of Masada is the chronicle of Josephus, a renegade Jew who wrote in Greek and whose work is not part

[1] The so-called "Masada complex" in modern Israel has been frequently mentioned and occasionally discussed. See, for example, Benjamin Kedar "*Tasbikh Maṣada*," in *Ha'aretz*, April 22, 1973, and Robert Alter, "The Masada Complex," in *Commentary*, July 1973, pp. 19-24. A paper entitled "From Yavneh to Masada," of which I have seen only a brief synopsis, was presented by Norman B. Mirsky of Cincinnati at the International Congress of Jewish Studies in Jerusalem in August 1973.

of the traditional Jewish cultural heritage.[2] There is a well-known Hebrew adaptation of Josephus made by an Italian Jew, probably in the 10th century, and widely read among Jews. It survives in many copies, was often reprinted, and was even translated into Judeo-Arabic, Judeo-Spanish, and more than once into Yiddish. The passages dealing with Masada seem, however, to have had little impact.[3]

Even more remarkably, the Persians had preserved no record of their founding father Cyrus—not even his name. Knowledge of this truly great ruler was due entirely to outside sources, in this case Jewish and Greek, and until very recently the Persians read neither the Bible nor the Greek historians, and knew even less of them than did the Jews of Josephus.[4]

There are similarities too in the manner and processes of the recovery of these two lost chapters of the past, with the same elements occurring in both cases. There is the visible impact of archaeology—

[2] Josephus, *The Jewish War*, vii, 252, 275, 280-406 (Loeb Classical Library edition, with an English translation by H. St. J. Thackeray, iii, pp. 576-577, 582-583, 584-619).

[3] Yosiphon, ed. H. Hominer, 3rd edition, Jerusalem 57/27/1967, pp. 260ff. On Yosiphon see M. Steinschneider, *Die Geschichts- literatur der Juden in Druckwerken und Handschriften*, i, Frankfurt (Verlag J. Kauffmann), 1905, § 19, pp. 25-33, and the standard Jewish encyclopaedias, s.v.

[4] For references to Cyrus see Pauly-Wissowa, *Realencyclopädie der classischen Altertumswissenschaft*, Stuttgart 1894ff. For a brief review of the place of Cyrus in classical history and myth see Antonio Pagliaro, *Ciro e l'impero persiano*, Rome (Accademia Nazionale dei Lincei), 1972.

for Cyrus the discovery and decipherment of a cylinder seal from Nineveh, now in the British Museum, which is the only contemporary record issuing from Cyrus himself, and, more striking, the massive ruins of Persepolis, the imperial capital of the ancient Persian monarchs of the line founded by Cyrus. For Masada there were the excavations at the site, and the double achievement of Professor Yigael Yadin in both recovering and popularizing this new chapter from Jewish history.[5]

The penetration of this new material into the popular consciousness from which it had completely disappeared again follows rather similar courses. On the Jewish side, it begins with the effort of Jewish scholarship, the famous *Jüdische Wissenschaft* of the German Jews, which drew extensively on Greek and Roman sources, unknown to Jewish traditional learning, to illuminate the hitherto obscure period of the Jewish struggle against Rome. This new information was more widely disseminated in the form of romantic novels, most of them written by German rabbis in their leisure moments, but also translated into Hebrew, in which form they had a considerable impact among the Jewish reading public in Eastern Europe.[6]

[5] See especially Yigael Yadin, *Masada: Herod's Fortress and the Zealots' Last Stand*, London (Weidenfeld and Nicolson), 1966.

[6] The most notable are Markus (Meyer) Lehmann (1831-1890), Ludwig Phillippson (1811-1889), Moses Wassermann, Herman Reckendorf (1825-1875), Salomo Kohn (1825-1904),

These novelists, though they dealt with several themes from the Roman period, do not seem to have been attracted by the fate of Masada. Even the historians content themselves with a brief account based on Josephus. The Christian travellers and archaeologists who in the course of the 19th century began to visit and to describe the site of Masada found no Jewish counterparts among Jewish residents and visitors and no impact on Jewish scholarship.[7]

Probably the most significant landmark in the restoration of Masada to the Jewish consciousness was the publication in 1927 of a poem under that name by the Hebrew poet, Yitzhak Lamdan. Lamdan was a survivor of the Russian revolution, the ensuing civil war, and the appalling pogroms in the Ukraine, which, until Hitler taught us otherwise, seemed to Jews the last word in horror and suffering. Arriving in Palestine, Lamdan clung to the slender hope presented by the small Jewish settlement of that time as the last hope and last refuge of Jewishness. He was well aware of the dangers and difficulties which confronted that settlement, and of its limited chance of surviving in a hostile world. Never-

---

and J. A. Francolm (1788-1849). They appear in most standard Jewish works of reference but have not, to my knowledge, yet formed the subject of a detailed study. On the Hebrew historical novel there is a brief article by David Patterson in *Sifrut* (London), i (1955), pp. 51-57.

[7] On these, see Yadin, *Masada*, pp. 239-255.

theless he felt very strongly—and the idea comes out again and again in this and other poems—that this was the last refuge and hope, and that if this failed there was nothing, nothing at all, for the Jews. Masada, no doubt known to him from scholarly and literary writings, provided him with a symbol, and a very appropriate one. The poem is apocalyptic in tone, full of dark portents of destruction and death. But interwoven with the theme of doom is one of hope, and the line "Masada shall not fall again" has become one of the most emotive slogans of modern Israel. The poem was enormously successful and ran through many editions.[8]

Cyrus too owed his return to the Persian consciousness to scholarship, to Persian translations of western books, to the first original Persian writings dealing with the ancient history of their country and to a succession of historical novels, the first of which was published in 1919, with Cyrus as hero. The informa-

[8] On Isaac Lamdan (1899-1954) see Leon I. Yudkin, *Isaac Lamdan, a Study in Twentieth-Century Hebrew Poetry*, London (East and West Library), 1971, and Alter, "The Masada Complex," p. 22. His poem *Masada* was first published in 1927, and has been reprinted many times. For English translations, see Yudkin, pp. 199-234, and excerpts in Ruth Finer Mintz, *Modern Hebrew Poetry: A Bilingual Anthology*, Berkeley and Los Angeles (Univ. of California Press) 1966, pp. 130ff., and A. Birman, *An Anthology of Modern Hebrew Poetry*, New York (Abelard-Schuman), 1968, pp. 148ff. The same mood is vividly expressed in another of Lamdan's poems, "The Green Dream" (English translation in A. Birman, pp. 153-154).

tion for these at first came exclusively from western sources, drawn ultimately from the Greeks and the Bible.[9]

Finally, in both cases the recovery and dissemination of this lost chapter of the past have a powerful ideological motivation—a new form of self-awareness, a new attempt at defining identity and aspiration, and hence the need to go beyond or beneath the inherited, traditional, and familiar past associated with the discredited self-image which leaders and rulers were seeking to abandon and replace.

[9] The first, *'Ishq u Salṭana*, "Love and Rule," was completed in 1916 by Shaykh Mūsā, principal of the Madrasa (religious seminary) in Hamadān. It was published in that city in 1919 and reprinted in Bombay in 1924-1925. The second, *Dāstān-i Bāstān yā Sarguzasht-i Kūrūsh*, "An Ancient Tale, or the Life of Cyrus," was the work of Ḥasan Khan Naṣratu'l-wizāra Badī'. Completed in 1920, it was published in Tehran in the following year. On the modern Persian historical novel, see B. Nikitine, "Le roman historique dans le littérature persane actuelle," in *Journal asiatique*, ccxxiii (1933), pp. 297-336—based in part on E. E. Berthels, "Persidskii istoričeskii roman XX veka," in *Problemy Literatury Vostoka*, i, *Trudi Instituta Vostokovedeniya Akademii Nauk SSSR*, i, Leningrad, 1932, pp. 111-126. A fuller account, not accessible to me, is that of Franciczek Machalski, *Historyczna Powieść Perska*, Cracow, 1952. See further E. G. Browne, *A History of Persian Literature in Modern Times* (A.D. 1500-1924), Cambridge (C.U.P.), 1924, pp. 464ff. and Jan Rypka and others, *History of Iranian Literature*, Dordrecht (Reidel), 1968, pp. 370, 372, 392-395. On modern Persian historiography relating to ancient history see C. A. Storey, *Persian Literature, a Bio-Bibliographical Survey*, ii/2, London (Luzac), 1936, pp. 246ff.; greatly expanded Russian translation by Y. E. Bregel, *Persidskaya Literatura*, ii, Moscow (Glavnaya Redaktsiya Vostočnoy Literatury), 1972, pp. 726ff.

Sometimes a new past, a new antiquity, are ready to hand in sources previously neglected or forgotten, in the discoveries of native or, more commonly, foreign scholars. Sometimes they are not ready to hand and have to be found or otherwise made available—exhumed, deciphered, or, if need be, invented. The English word "invent," it will be recalled, comes from a Latin verb meaning "to find," and the "Discovery of the True Cross" is known to Christians as *inventio crucis*, still commemorated under that name. It is significant that the discoverer of the True Cross, according to Christian legend, was St. Helena, the mother of Constantine, the emperor who made the Roman Empire Christian and launched the history of both Rome and Christendom on new paths. A new future required a different past.

There are many ways of defining and subdividing history; traditionally, by who, and when, and where; then, in a more sophisticated age, by topic—by what, and how, and, for the intellectually ambitious, why; methodologically, by types of sources and the manner of their use; ideologically, by function and purpose—of the historian more than of the history, and many others. The classification used here, as will have emerged from the above remarks, is into three types, as follows:

(1) Remembered history. This consists of statements about the past, rather than history in the strict sense, and ranges from the personal recollections claimed by the elders to the living traditions of a civilization, as embodied in its scriptures, its classics,

and its inherited historiography. It may be described as the collective memory of a community or nation or other entity—what it, or its rulers and leaders, poets, and sages, choose to remember as significant, both as reality and symbol.

(2) Recovered history. This is the history of events and movements, of persons and ideas, that have been forgotten, that is to say, at some stage and for some reason rejected by the communal memory, and then, after a longer or shorter interval, recovered by academic scholarship—by the study of records, the excavation of buried cities, the decipherment of forgotten scripts and languages, and the consequent reconstruction of a forgotten past. But reconstruction begs the basic question, and disguises what would be better described as construction. The word itself indicates the dangers of the process, and leads us to the third type of history.

(3) Invented history. This is history for a purpose, a new purpose differing from previous purposes. It may be invented in either the Latin or the English sense of the word, devised and interpreted from remembered and recovered history where feasible, and fabricated where not.

Remembered history of one kind or another is common to all human groups from the primitive tribe to the universal empire, from the tribal cult to the universal church. It embodies poetic and symbolic truth as understood by the people, even where it is inaccurate in detail, but it becomes false or is rejected as false when the desired self-image changes and the remembered past no longer corresponds to it or supports it. It is preserved in commemorative ceremonies and monuments, religious and later secular, and in the words and rituals associated with them—in pageantry and drama, song and recitation, chronicle and biography, epic and ballad and their modern equivalents, also in official celebrations, popular entertainment, and elementary education.

Recovered history is the result of the discovery and reassessment of the past by critical scholarship—basically a modern and European task. The ancients, with few exceptions, were not interested in ancient history;[10] indeed most history, until the new curiosity of the Renaissance, was either remembered or contemporary and much of it still purposive.

The invention of history is no new invention. It is an ancient practice dating back to remote antiquity and directed to a variety of purposes. Again, it is common to all groups, ranging in type from the primitive heroic myths of nomadic tribes to Soviet official historiography or American revisionism.

Let us now return to our two examples, Masada and Cyrus, and look beyond them to the problems

[10] See for example the remarks of A. Momigliano on Herodotus in his article "The Place of Herodotus in the History of Historiography," in *History*, xliii (1958), pp. 1-13. Reprinted in idem, *Studies in Historiography*, New York (Harper & Row), 1966, pp. 127-142.

Wingate College Library

they raise in the study of Jewish and of Perso-Islamic history respectively.

The Jewish interest in and attitude to history goes through several phases. The first is that of the Old Testament, where history is of basic importance. From then until now the very core of the Jewish identity is established by a sequence of historical events—the career of Abraham and his migration from Ur of the Chaldees to Egypt, the exodus of the Jewish tribes from Egypt, the revelation of the Law on Mount Sinai, the entry of the Jews to the Promised Land, and their adventures under the judges and the kings thereafter. The historical books and even the non-historical books of the Old Testament make the religious purpose of history quite clear. "Thou shalt not be afraid of them: but shalt remember what the Lord thy God did unto Pharaoh, and unto Egypt; the great temptations which thine eyes saw, and the signs, and the wonders, and the mighty hand, and the stretched out arm, whereby the Lord thy God brought thee out: so shall the Lord thy God do unto all the people of whom thou art afraid" (Deuteronomy VII: 18-19). And again: "Remember the days of old, consider the years of many generations: ask thy father, and he will show thee; thy elders, and they will tell thee . . ." (Deuteronomy XXXII: 7). Psalm 105 is almost entirely historical. "Seek the Lord, and His strength; seek His face evermore. Remember His marvellous works that He has done; His wonders, and the judgment of His mouth;

O ye seed of Abraham, His servant, ye children of
Jacob, His chosen. He is the Lord our God: His
judgments are in all the earth. He hath remembered
His covenant for ever, the word which He com-
manded to a thousand generations. Which covenant
He made with Abraham, and His oath unto Isaac;
and He confirmed the same unto Jacob for a law,
and unto Israel for an everlasting covenant. . . ."

The Isaiah of the restoration after the Babylonian
captivity—a time of significant political and religious
changes—also urges the study of history for encour-
agement and self-awareness. "Hearken to me, ye that
follow after righteousness, ye that seek the Lord;
look unto the rock whence you are hewn, and to the
hole of the pit whence you are digged. Look unto
Abraham your father and unto Sarah that bare you;
for I called him alone and blessed him, and increased
him" (Isaiah LI: 1-2).

These themes are emphasized by the Chroniclers,
the Psalmists, and the Prophets alike. They are re-
peated in the daily prayers and commemorated by
the festivals of the Jewish year. For the Jews, their
ancient history is of fundamental importance, and
remains so until the destruction of Judah. Until then,
the major events are recorded in the books of the
Old Testament. True, they appear in various versions
representing different phases of the growing historiographic sophistication of the ancient Hebrews,
and also reflecting various viewpoints—tribal, royal,
priestly, and prophetic. Nevertheless they are all at

one in believing in the importance of "knowing the rock whence you are hewn, and the hole of the pit whence you are digged." The location of the pit and the composition of the rock have, however, given rise to some disagreement.

The period of the second temple brings a marked change in attitude, manifested in various ways. The Old Testament records the restoration of the Jews from the Babylonian captivity to the land of Israel, and the building of the new temple, but tells us very little of historical events after that. There is no narrative of political and military events like that of the earlier period, and there are only two historical festivals, both minor, Purim and Hanukka. Only the first of these rates a book in the Old Testament, and was included in the canon, we are told, after some doubts and hesitations.[11] The latter is not represented at all.[12]

[11] See Talmud, *Mo'ed, Megilla*, 7a, 14a; Jerusalem Talmud, *Megilla*, 7od.

[12] When the memory of the Hasmonean kings and the hostility against them had both receded into the past, a short Hebrew version of an account of the Maccabean victories, known as *Megillat Benê Ḥashmonay*, for a while acquired some popularity and was read in synagogues during Hanukka. Rabbi Nissim ben Ya'qōv of Qayrawān even mentions such a work on a par with the Megilla of Esther (The Arabic Original of Ibn Shâhîn's *Book of Comfort* . . . , ed. Julian Obermann, New Haven [Yale Univ. Press], 1933, p. 4; Hebrew translation by J. W. Hirschberg, *Ḥibbûr Yafê Me-ha-yeshû'a*, Jerusalem 5714 [1964], p. 3 of text, cf. introduction, pp. 58-59. Cf. Abraham Kehana, *Sifrût ha-Historia ha-Yisra'elit*, Warsaw, 5692 [1922-1923], i, pp. 14ff., and M. Gaster, "The Scroll of the Hasmoneans," in *Transactions*

Purim is a festival of a new type—the first diaspora festival, almost medieval in character. It is concerned with Jews living as a minority in exile under alien rule, at the mercy of a good king or a wicked counsellor, saved by what later became the classic form of intercession on their behalf by men or women with influence at court—what the Jewish tradition calls *Shtadlanut*, a combination of pleading, intercession, persuasion, inducement, and good offices, by those who have reached a position where they can help their people in this way. The book of Esther might be described as the proof-text of *Shtadlanut*, of a tradition developing from Esther and Mordecai at the court of Shushan, through Maimonides at the court of the Cairo Sultanate, to the Jewish lobbyists in Washington in our day.

Hanukka has no anchorage in the canon, not even a *megilla* like Esther, though attempts were made at a later date to give a short Hebrew account of the Maccabean victories such a status. They did not succeed. Nowadays it is fashionable to treat Hanukka as the commemoration of a great Jewish political and military victory—a successful struggle for independence against foreign rule, and it has become customary for Hanukka parties at Israeli embassies to be given by the defense attaché. This was not the traditional interpretation of the significance of Hanukka.

of the 9th International Congress of Orientalists, part ii, 1893, pp. 1-32).

The rabbis seem to have made a conscious effort to depoliticize and to demilitarize this festival, laying their main stress on its purely religious aspect, the miracle of the lights, and paying little attention to the Maccabees and their military victories.

One can even speak of a systematic downgrading of the Maccabees and their Hasmonean successors by the rabbis. History books were written under the Hasmonean monarchy but, significantly, they were not preserved by the Jews. They survive in Greek translation because the Maccabees were retrospectively adopted as saints and heroes by the Christian church. The books of the Maccabees form part of the Apocrypha, accepted in the Catholic canon but not in the Jewish. The Hebrew or Aramaic originals are lost and the apocryphal Greek translations were unknown to the Jewish tradition. Rabbinic literature is not concerned with history as such, and even expresses a certain mistrust. References to the history of the time are few and on the whole uninformative.

The reason is not far to seek. One of the basic purposes of historiography is to legitimize authority —and authority in Judaism was now shifting to the rabbis and leaving the priesthood and the monarchy. The Hasmoneans embodied both of these at the same time, and the later monarchs betrayed Judaism by adopting the very Hellenistic civilization against which Judas Maccabeus and his brothers had fought. It is significant that of the two great rabbinic corpuses, those of Jerusalem and of Babylon, the more authoritative and the more respected is that of Babylon, i.e. that which grew up under Persian and not under Jewish jurisdiction.

Another point is of importance. The rabbis were custodians of the oral law, and claimed their authority as such. For them therefore an historical approach to law was dangerous, for by querying the source of the oral law and exposing its development, it could call their authority into account or even dangerously undermine it.

A new phase set in after the destruction of the temple and of the Jewish state, when all these factors became clearer. Priestly and royal competition were now removed, and the rabbis were in uncontested control, their authority now institutionalized through the patriarchate in Palestine, then the gaonate in Babylon and their successors elsewhere. Rabbinical interest in historiography was minimal, and was concerned only to establish the legitimacy of the oral law and of its authorized exponents. Their historical approach is exemplified in stories of the revelation of the oral law to Moses on Sinai, giving it equal authority and contemporaneity with the written law, and by a series of narratives containing chains of transmission, best exemplified in *Pirqe Abhoth*. "Moses received the Torah on Sinai and transmitted it to Joshua, Joshua to the elders, and the elders to the prophets, and the prophets to the men of the great synagogue. The latter used to say three things: be patient in the administration of justice, rear many

disciples and make a fence around the Torah" (Ch.
i, Mishna i). This puts the authority and the purpose of "the men of the great synagogue" and their
successors in a nutshell. Neither kings nor priests,
it will be noted, have any place in this sequence.

As so often, the collective memory caught and
retained one dramatic episode, to which it gave a
great and symbolic significance. The Talmudic literature, usually so sparing of historical narrative detail,
offers no less than five full versions, apart from
numerous mentions, of the story of how Rabbi Yohanan ben Zakkai escaped from the beleaguered and
doomed city of Jerusalem, made his way to the camp
of the Roman commander Vespasian, and obtained
from him, as a boon, permission to establish a rabbinical college in the little coastal town of Yavne,
which thereafter became the center of the rabbinical
patriarchate. According to some versions, Yohanan
ben Zakkai was able to elude the vigilance of the
zealots and leave the city by pretending to fall sick
and then die, whereupon his living body was carried
in a coffin by his faithful disciples and taken outside
the walls, ostensibly for burial, in fact to the Roman
camp.[13] Traditional historians have seen in this the
triumph of the spirit over the sword, of Jerusalem
over Rome, of God's law over worldly might. More

[13] For an analysis of the different versions, see Gedalyahu
Alon, *Meḥqarim be-Toldot Yisra'el*, i, Tel Aviv (Ha-Kibbutz
ha-Meuhad), 1967, pp. 219-252. See further Jacob Neusner, *A
Life of Yohanan ben Zakkai ca. 1-80 C.E.*, 2nd edition, Leiden
(Brill), 1970, pp. 157ff.

concretely, they have seen in Rabbi Yohanan and his disciples and successors the preservers of Jewish identity and guarantors of Jewish survival, at a time when the state, the temple, the city, and the land, on which these had hitherto depended, were all being lost. Some modern critics, less concerned with religious values, have found a bitter appropriateness in Rabbi Yohanan's survival disguised as a corpse. Others have reminded the Jews that it is from that corpse and his bearers that, figuratively speaking, they are all descended, and not from the heroic defenders of Masada. Those had no descendants.[14]

Only one military episode receives some attention in the Rabbinic literature—the unsuccessful revolt of Simon Bar-Kokhba against the Romans in A.D. 132-135. The reason is clear enough. Bar-Kokhba enjoyed the support of 'Aqīva, one of the greatest of the Rabbis, and of many other Rabbis and scholars. Ten of them, including 'Aqīva, were tortured and executed by the Romans, and are venerated in the Rabbinic tradition as martyrs. Bar-Kokhba himself is accorded scant respect, and in some passages is even condemned as a liar and an impostor. He had no Josephus, and his career is known only from external sources, from rabbinical mentions, and from coins and other remains.

Jewish historiographic literature in the Middle Ages is sparse and poor. In this respect it is in striking contrast with earlier Jewish historical writing, with

[14] I owe this observation to Dr. Arthur Hertzberg.

non-Jewish contemporary historical writing, both Christian and more especially Islamic, and even with Jewish literature on other subjects. Jewish historical writing is on a far lower intellectual level than that of either the surrounding society in which the Jews lived or of Jewish scholarship in other fields.

It is basically of two or possibly three types, all functional. The first is martyrology, records of massacres and persecutions, the purpose of which is to stiffen the endurance of the survivors. The second is the history of scholarship, the succession of rabbis and the filiation of pupils and teachers. The purpose here is clearly to legitimize the authority of the rabbis, especially against the Samaritans, Karaites, and other challengers. The best example of this type is the *Sefer ha-Qabbala* of Abraham ben Da'ud (written in 1160-1161), tracing the chain of transmission from antiquity through the patriarchs of Palestine, the gaonim of Babylon, and then the branches which brought the rabbinic tradition to Egypt, to north Africa, and to Spain.[15]

A third variety, which is only marginally historiographical, is the literature of prediction—the apocalyptic writings which tell the past in the form of a prediction of the future and claim to foretell the coming of Messiah. Examples of this kind of writing

[15] Abraham ibn Daud, *The Book of Tradition*, edited and translated by Gerson D. Cohen, London (Routledge & Kegan Paul), 1967.

are already to be found in the Old and New Testaments; there are many of them among the Midrashim and related writings.

Why? What is the reason for this feebleness of the medieval Jewish historian, whether we contrast him with his own Jewish predecessors, with his own non-Jewish contemporaries, or with his Jewish contemporaries engaged in other fields of scholarship?

One reason is the lack of a focus. In ancient and medieval times history required some sort of focus, a country, a state, or a dynasty, even perhaps an institution, but not of an idea, a theme, or a topic. Jewish historians lacked a focus of a familiar type. Hence, they also lacked a patron or a sponsor, someone to commission and pay for the historical writing —and historians too must live. More important was the absence of any real need. The religiously vital history of the Jewish people was already fixed in scripture, liturgy, and calendar. Subsequent needs were minimal, and were met by martyrologies and rabbinical chains of transmission.

The poverty of Jewish historiography is due not just to neglect but to positive rejection. The great theologian, jurist, and philosopher Maimonides advised his Jewish readers against "books found among the Arabs describing historical events, the governments of kings and Arab genealogy, or books of song and similar works, which neither possess wisdom nor yield profit for the body, but are merely a waste of time."[16] Incidentally, Maimonides himself refers frequently in his religious and legal writings to the history of the Old Testament period, but very rarely to that of the Maccabees and after. On this his information is fragmentary, and appears to derive exclusively from rabbinical sources.

Maimonides' rejection of history expresses a fairly general view among medieval Jewish scholars. In this respect there is a striking similarity between the Jewish attitude and that of the Shi'ite Muslims in their approach to history. For Sunni Muslims history was of tremendous, indeed of transcendent, importance. Their faith began with the mission of the Prophet—an event in history. The circumstances and meaning of revelation could be known to subsequent generations only through memory and record, through the work, that is to say, of preservation and transmission of the first historians of Islam. The *Sunna,* the Muslim equivalent of the oral law of Judaism, was essentially historical in character. According to Muslim doctrine, divine guidance passed, after the death of the Prophet, to the Muslim community as a whole, and the consensus of the community—that is, the precedents set by its leaders and

[16] Commentary on *M. Sanhedrin*, x, 1, ed. J. Holzer, *Zur Geschichte der Dogmenlehre in der jüdischen religionsphilosophie des Mittelalters: Mose Maimuni's Einleitung zu Chelek*, Berlin (Poppelauer), 1901. Translated by S. W. Baron, "The Historical Outlook of Maimonides," in *Proceedings of the American Academy of Jewish Research*, vi (1934-1935), pp. 7-8; cf. idem, *History*, vi, 199.

teachers—are themselves a revelation of God's will
on earth. God in the Muslim view would not allow
His community to fall into sin. What the community
as a whole accepted therefore was right and what
it did was an expression of God's purpose. The
Sunna of Islam, the consensus of the community,
was known by tradition, and the study of tradition,
which provided the basis of Muslim theology and
of Muslim law, is essentially historical in method.
Seen in this way, the study of history played an essential role in the most important of all tasks—the
preparation in this life for the next.[17]

The Shi'ite view was completely different. After
the murder of 'Alī, who for the Shi'ites was the
only rightful caliph after the Prophet, the remaining
caliphs were all usurpers, and history had taken a
wrong turning. The Muslim community was, so to
speak, living in sin, in a kind of Islamic equivalent
of the Jewish Galut, even of the Shekhina in Galut,
the Divine Presence in Exile. For the Shi'a, the actions of usurping rulers, the rulings of heretical jurists, had no value and no significance. Shi'ite historiography is in consequence poor by comparison with
Sunni historiography and is preoccupied with concerns similar to those of the Jews—with the sufferings
of the Shi'ite martyrs, with the chain of transmission
of the Shi'ite leaders, the Imāms, and with the signs

[17] On this, see further Bernard Lewis, *Islam from the Prophet
Muhammad to the Capture of Constantinople*, i, New York
(Harper & Row), 1974, pp. xviiff.

and portents of the coming of the Mahdī, the messianic figure who for them, as for the Jews, would
bring history back to its proper path and establish the
will of God upon earth.[18]

Jewish curiosity about their own and general history was, however, not entirely lacking in medieval
times. Abraham ibn Da'ūd was concerned to fit Jewish history into the framework of general history,
thus echoing the concern of the earliest Christian
historians to synchronize biblical and classical chro-
nologies. The popularity of Yosiphon—the one genu-
inely historical Jewish work of the Middle Ages—
illustrates this interest. But the real beginning of
Jewish historiography came with the Renaissance—
with the new humanism, the new curiosity, and the
new contacts which allowed external influences to
penetrate the ghetto and affect Jewish life and scholarship. Such figures as Joseph ha-Cohen (1495-1575)
and Samuel Usque (d. after 1553) wrote martyrologies like their medieval predecessors, but they did so
in a new way and with new concepts.[19] Joseph ha-

[18] Cf. B. Lewis, *op. cit.*, pp. ii, 50ff.

[19] On Joseph ha-Cohen see M. Waxman, *A History of Jewish
Literature*, ii, New York (Yoseloff), 1933, pp. 474-476; Steinschneider, *Geschichtsliteratur*, pp. 101-103. Samuel Usque wrote
in Portuguese. His *Consolation for the Tribulations of Israel*
was published in the original by Mendes dos Romedios, 3 vols.,
Coimbra, 1906, and in an annotated English translation by Mar-
tin A. Cohen in Philadelphia (Jewish Publication Society of
America), 1965.

Cohen also tackled general history and wrote a chronicle of the kings of the Turks and the Franks.[20] Venetian and Turkish history also occupied the attention of the Cretan Jewish historian—or rather gossip-writer—Eliyahu Kapsali (ca. 1490-1555).[21] These, however, remained primitive and credulous by comparison with the Christian historians of the Renaissance period and it is clear that they are not the products of any great historiographic tradition.

A new phase began with the writings of Azariah de' Rossi (1514-1577),[22] a 16th-century Italian Jew who was the first to apply the critical European method and approach to Jewish studies and to try and deal with ancient and early medieval Jewish history using non-Jewish sources and scholarly analysis as well as Jewish scripture, rabbinic writings, and tradition. For this reason he was very much disapproved of by the rabbis, who saw in his approach

---

[20] *Divre ha-yamim le-mulkhê Tsarfat u-vêt Ottoman ha-Toger*, printed in Sabionetta in 1554, and in several later editions. There is a very inaccurate English translation by C. H. F. Bialloblotzky, *The Chronicles of Rabbi Joseph ben Joshua ben Meir, the Sphardi*, 2 vols., London (Oriental Translation Fund), 1835-1836. For Ottoman history Rabbi Joseph relies mainly on Italian sources, and especially on Giovanni Maria Angiolello of Vicenza, whom he cites as Vicentino (cf. English translation, i, p. 275).

[21] On Kapsali see Steinschneider, *Geschichtsliteratur*, pp. 93-94; Waxman, *History*, ii, p. 474. A complete edition of his Turkish history is now in press in Israel.

[22] On Azariah de' Rossi see Steinschneider, *Geschichtsliteratur*, p. 107; Waxman, *History*, ii, pp. 516-522; S. Bernfeld, *Benê 'Aliya*, Tel Aviv (Dvir), 1930, pp. 135-153.

a danger to the faith, or if not to the faith then to their own position in it. This attitude continued through the great subsequent development of Jewish scholarship in the 19th century and even into modern times, when, for example, the American scholar Haim Tchernovitz,[23] who wrote under the name of Rav Tsa'ir, published a history of the *Shulhan Arukh* and of the *Halakha*, the rabbinic law, and was severely reproved for his pains by some rabbis, who felt that the very idea of a history of the *Halakha*—that is to say, of admitting the notion of change and development and the even more ominous possibility of criticism—was itself suspect and dangerous.

Despite this kind of opposition, however, Jewish scholarship continued, especially in Germany, and was carried on by now by men with a sound classical and general education. One important result of this was the recovery for Jewish readers of the history of the second temple—of the Maccabees, the Hasmonean monarchy and after, the Jewish wars against Rome, and the events of the early Christian centuries. For all of these the main historical sources are non-Jewish or preserved in non-Jewish languages and had therefore been unknown to traditional scholars and their flocks. Most of these new scholars were themselves rabbis and pious Jews, but they were also

[23] On Hayyim Tchernowitz see Waxman, *History*, iv, pp. 1126-1128.

19th-century Europeans, chiefly Germans, with a characteristic interest in political and military affairs and a tendency to see history as the history of the state and of the actions of statesmen. Jost, Herzfeld, and Graetz in Germany, Derenbourg in France, made important progress in this field, and found their echoes also in the rather poorer Hebrew historiography of the late 19th and early 20th centuries in the writings of such scholars as Isaac Halevi and Wolf Yavetz, who mark the transition from traditional to scholarly learning and who exercised very considerable influence on the new generation of Jewish intellectuals in eastern Europe.[24]

This refashioning of attitudes towards certain epochs of the Jewish past was accomplished not only through scholarly writing but also through fiction and, in particular, through a whole school of romantic historical novels. Most of these were German, a few English, but many were translated into Hebrew and widely read in eastern Europe. *The Vale of Cedars* by Grace Aguilar, *Alroy* by Disraeli, *Daniel Deronda* by George Eliot, all had their effect, as did a series of German rabbinical novelists such as Marcus Lehmann, Moses Wassermann, Ludwig Philippson, and others. Of particular influence was Hermann Reckendorf, whose work, adapted into Hebrew under the title *Zikhronot le-Bait David* (Memories of

[24] See Waxman, *History*, iii, pp. 424ff. (on "Jewish Science"); iv, pp. 720ff.

the House of David), exercised great influence on Jewish readers in eastern Europe.[25]

At first, the outlook of these was still rabbinic. Their heroes were Ben Zakkai and the men of Yavneh, not the defenders of Masada, 'Aqīva rather than Bar Kokhba. But a gradual change came with the rise of Zionism and still more so with the development of the Jewish Yishuv and the establishment of the Jewish state in Israel. All this led to an increasingly anxious quest for roots, for a historical background to the Jewish identity as a territorial nation, to statehood; at a lower level, also, for military heroes and, above all, for political, national, and territorial continuity, spanning the vast gulf of diaspora and restoring the chain of transmission from the rabbinate, which had held it since the collapse of the Herodian monarchy, to the state. The national passion for archaeology in Israel today is an expression of the same urgent need to find roots, literally in the soil.

Jewish self-image and its historiographic reflection were transformed by the destruction of the state and temple and the exile of the Jewish people. But continuity was preserved in language and scripture, memory and commemoration. The rabbis were not only the supplanters but also the heirs and custodians of the old tradition from which they claimed to derive their own legitimacy. The situation in Persia and

[25] See Waxman, *History*, iv, p. 160.

in other Middle Eastern countries was radically different. Here the conquest and conversion of these peoples to Islam brought radical change and, above all, discontinuity. Muslim conquest brought a new religion and the consequent changes were far greater than, for example, in Christendom. Christianity triumphed in the Roman Empire, but it did so by conversion, not by conquest, and it preserved the Roman state and the Roman law and learned to live with the Latin and Greek heritage. Islam created its own state, the Caliphate, and brought its own language, Arabic, and its own scripture, the Qur'ān. The old states were destroyed. The old languages and even the old scripts were forgotten. The rupture was not as complete as was once thought, or as Muslims claimed, and much pre-Islamic custom survived under an Islamic veneer. Islam was by no means unaware of pre-Islamic antiquity but limited its borrowings to what it considered usable knowledge—philosophy, medicine, science, mathematics, and the like—things which were useful for helping the body in this world and preparing the soul for the next. There was no usable past from a Muslim point of view—hence the Muslim neglect both of history and of epic, with only minor exceptions. There was thus complete discontinuity in the self-image, the corporate sense of identity, and the collective memory of the Islamic peoples of the Middle East.[26]

[26] See F. Rosenthal, *Das Fortleben der Antike im Islam*, Zürich and Stuttgart (Artemis), 1965.

For the Muslim, the community to which he belongs is Islam. The history which concerns him is that of the Prophet, the caliphs, and their successors. His heroes are the warriors in the holy wars of Islam, even if their victories were won over his own pagan or Christian ancestors. Significant history begins with the advent of Islam; pre-Islamic history survives only in two forms: the first, and by far the most important, through the elements of biblical and ancient Arabian history encapsulated in the Qur'ān and tradition; the second, and less important, consisting of the local memories or records of the *immediately* preceding period, notably in Arabia and Persia. The rest was discarded. The Sasanids, the Persian monarchy overthrown by the Arab conquerors, were to some extent remembered in Arabic historiography. The older history was utterly forgotten—the Achaemenids and Parthians of Persia, the Assyrians and Babylonians of Iraq, the Aramaeans and Phoenicians of Syria and Lebanon; even the Pharaohs of Egypt were unknown, their records locked in an unknown script and a dead language, their massive monuments neglected or deliberately defaced, their very names forgotten, except for the Pharaoh of the Exodus, who appears in the Qur'ān as villain of a story which has Moses as its hero.[27]

[27] Qur'ān, x, 76/75ff.; xxvi, 9/10ff.; xxviii, passim; xliv, 16/17ff., and numerous allusions. See further *Encyclopaedia of Islam*, second edition, s.vv. "Banū Isrā'īl" (by S. D. Goitein) and "Fir'awn" (by A. J. Wensinck and G. Vajda), where further references are given.

The restoration of the ancient past was the work of the 19th and 20th centuries. At the beginning of the 19th century, all that the world knew of the history of the ancient Middle East was what preserved in Greek and Hebrew, that is to say by the only two peoples active in the ancient Middle East who had preserved continuity of identity into modern times, and who had retained and could still read their ancient writings. This history was part of their collective memory and was passed by them, with their scriptures and classics, to Christendom—but not to Islam, for Muslims read neither the Bible nor the classics. The name of Cyrus was well known in medieval Europe and appears even in the sagas of faraway Iceland. It does not appear in Islam, not even in Persia, where the pre-Islamic past was rejected and literally buried. The recovery was for long the work of European, later also of Russian and American, scholars, and was only gradually accepted by the Muslims of the Middle East.

The process began in Egypt with the decipherment of the Rosetta Stone and then of other ancient Egyptian writings, and the consequent recovery of several millennia of ancient Egyptian history. This coincided with two other important developments. One was the growth of western education and hence greater access to western writings and greater openness to influence by western concepts, including concepts of national identity. This enabled Egyptians to learn of the western notion of the ethnic and territorial nation and to see themselves for the first time as a continuing millennial entity before and after their conversion to other religions, first to Christianity and then to Islam. The second favoring circumstance was the emergence in Egypt of a local autonomous dynasty, that of the Khedives, with separatist ambitions and thus with a practical motive for encouraging the notion of Egypt as an historical and political entity, i.e. as a nation in the European sense and therefore, in accordance with current views, entitled to express its nationhood in statehood.

The history of pharaonic Egypt was first made available to Egyptians in Arabic by Shaykh Rifāʿa Rāfiʿ al-Taḥtāwī, a graduate of al-Azhar who had spent a few years in Paris and who, in 1868, published a history of Egypt covering the period of the ancient Egyptians, the Pharaohs, the Ptolemies, the Romans, and the Byzantines, and ending where Egyptian history under the Muslims had usually begun— with the Arab Conquest. This book was the first of its kind, and marked a turning point not only in the writing of history in Egypt but also in the Egyptians' awareness of themselves as a nation.[28] Thereafter, with the progress of archaeology, the uncovering of more remains, and the decipherment of more texts, pharaonic Egypt loomed larger and larger in the

[28] See Gamal el-Din el-Shayyal, *A History of Egyptian Historiography in the Nineteenth Century*, Alexandria (Alexandria Univ. Press), 1962, especially pp. 23ff.

Egyptian self-image and set up a continuing tension
in the Egyptian psyche between the two personalities, the one Egyptian, the other Arab-Islamic, each
with a different identity, a different memory, a different past. This tension is dramatized by the Quranic
version of the Exodus story in which Pharaoh appears as oppressor and the Banū Isrā'īl, the children
of Israel, under their leader and prophet Moses, Mūsā,
are the heroes—and more than the heroes, the fa-
vored of God and the recipients of God's guidance on
earth. This tension is accentuated at the present time,
when the heirs of the Pharaohs find themselves at
war with the heirs of the Banū Isrā'īl. An Egyptian
woman writer, who uses the pen-name of Bint al-
Shāṭi'—the daughter of the (Nile) river bank—
went so far as to write an article immediately before
the Six Day War, implying that the Qur'ān had got
it wrong and that Pharaoh was right after all. Nebu-
chadnezzar gets an honorable mention too.[29]

In other Arabic-speaking countries, the reaction to
the recovered ancient past was later, slower, and, on
the whole, politically less significant. The Iraqis paid
some attention to Assyria and Babylon, but did not
identify themselves with them to the extent the Egyptians did with the Pharaohs. In Lebanon, the Phoeni-

[29] Bint al-Shāṭi', "Al-Ab'ād al-ta'rīkhiyya li-hādhihi 'l-ma'raka"
(The Historical Dimensions of This Struggle), *al-Ahrām*, June
2, 1967; English translation in *Midstream*, xv (6), June-July
1969, pp. 61-63; cf. S. Shamir, "The Attitude of Arab Intellectuals to the Six-Day War," in *The Anatomy of Peace in the
Middle East*, New York (1969), pp. 6ff.

cians were claimed more particularly by the Maronites and were therefore denounced by the Muslims as representing an anti-Arab or anti-pan-Arab force. A parallel situation arose in Syria, where a body called the Syrian Popular Party put forward a program of Syrian as distinct from Arab nationalism, and claimed to have its roots in the ancient Aramaic culture of Syria. As a result of this, even to show an interest in Aramaic civilization can be hazardous, since it lays one open to the suspicion of being a supporter of the Syrian Popular Party, now illegal.

During the heyday of pan-Arabism a solution to this problem was found by the retroactive posthumous naturalization of all the ancient Semitic peoples, except one, as Arabs. This served several purposes. In the first place, it accentuated and underpinned the Arab identity of these countries and countered any dangerous tendencies towards what they contemptuously called the "pharaonism" of the Egyptians and its analogues elsewhere. In the second place, it extended the time-span of Arabism by millennia and vastly increased the Arab contribution to humanity, by claiming for it the achievements of all, or nearly all, the Semitic peoples of the ancient orient. In the third place, it set an early date on Arab claims to the Middle East—and, in particular, by claiming the Canaanites as Arabs, was even able to produce an Arab claim to Palestine antedating the first Israelite settlement. It had a further use in that, through the Carthaginians, it served to extend the range of ancient Arabism even to North Africa. Since, according to this doctrine, the ancient Semites, apart from the Israelites who are still extant and therefore excluded, were all Arabs, the great Islamic expansion of the 7th and 8th centuries was not a conquest but a liberation, and indeed is so presented in schoolbooks —as the liberation of Arabs from Persian, Byzantine, and other imperialisms.[30]

In recent years, with the decline of pan-Arabism, there has been some reaction against this. In Egypt there has been a marked revival of Egyptian, as distinct from Arab, identity and even in the countries of the Fertile Crescent and North Africa there has been more talk of Phoenicians, Arameans, Cartha-

[30] See Anwar G. Chejne, "The Use of History by Modern Arab Writers," in *Middle East Journal* (1960), pp. 394ff., where Arabic examples are cited. On the "Arab" Canaanites, see Isḥāq Mūsā al-Ḥusaynī, *'Urūbat Bayt al-Maqdis*, Beirut (Palestine Liberation Organization), 1969, and Muhammad Adīb al-'Amin, *'Urūbat Falastīn*, Beirut (al-Maktaba al-Asriyya), 1972; on their settlement in North Africa, the civilizing mission of Carthage ("the first democratic state in the world"), and their struggle against Roman imperialism, see Ahmad Tawfiq al-Madanī, *Hādhihi hiya al-Jazā'ir*, Cairo (Nahda), 1956, pp. 45ff. For a political example, see the treatise *La question palestinienne*, published by a Colloquium of Arab jurists held in Algiers in July 1967, pp. 22-24. On the clash of conflicting historical self-images in Arab countries (and elsewhere) see David C. Gordon, *Self-Determination and History in the Third World*, Princeton, N.J. (Princeton Univ. Press), 1971; G. E. von Grunebaum, *Modern Islam: the Search for Cultural Identity*, Berkeley and Los Angeles (Univ. of California Press), 1962; Wilfred Cantwell Smith, *Islam in Modern History*, Princeton, N.J. (Princeton Univ. Press), 1957.

ginians, and the like. Much of this however has been
surreptitious and cultural rather than overtly political, for pan-Arabism, even in its decline, remains the
only publicly and safely avowable ideology. The only
overt resistance to it has come from a group of poets
who call themselves, significantly, al-Rāfiḍūn, the
refusers, and whose verses reveal a desire to go back
beyond the Arab Conquest and seek ancient roots in
an earlier identity.[31] In this they offer a close parallel
with the so-called "Canaanites" in modern Israel and
their predecessor, the poet Saul Tchernikhovsky, who
looked back with yearning to a pagan secular Jewish
nation before the rise of historic Judaism.[32]

In Turkey there was a special problem of not two,
but three, pasts. The remembered past was the familiar Ottoman Islamic one, based on the history of
the Ottoman Empire and its immediate predecessors,
the empires of medieval Islam. This was the common, corporate recollection of the Ottoman Turkish
people, embodied in their schoolbooks, their poems,
their literature, and their self-awareness. The recovered history of the 19th and 20th centuries led them

[31] See Muḥammad al-Nuwayhī, "Difāʿ ʿan shuʿarāʾ al-rafḍ," in
Al-Risāla, September 1, 1964, pp. 14-18; idem (Mohamed al-
Nowaihi), "The Battle of the New Poetry," in *Texas Quarterly*,
ix/2 (1966), pp. 148-157.

[32] See Eisig Selberschlag, *Saul Tschernikhovsky, Poet of Revolt*,
London (East and West Library), 1968, pp. 36ff. On the "Canaanites" of the 1950's see Barukh Kurzweil, "Mahutah u-meqoro-
têhah shel tenuʿat ha-ʿIvrim ha-tseʿirim," in *Luaḥ Ha'aretz* (Tel
Aviv, 1952), pp. 107-129.

in two different and divergent directions. On the one hand, there was the local history of Turkey before the coming of the Turks—the ancient peoples and civilizations of Anatolia going back to Hittite times, but of course excluding the Greeks and Armenians, who shared with the Jews the disadvantage of still being extant and therefore not claimable as glorious ancestors. A second direction was the history of the Turks before they came to Turkey, and this led to central Asian studies and to the whole field of early Turkic history. The political equivalents of these were, on the one hand, patriotism, that is to say loyalty by country; on the other, pan-Turkism, the nationalist doctrine of the common identity of all the Turkish-speaking peoples. Among the Arabs it was pan-Arabism rather than local patriotism which has for long been dominant, though its influence has now begun to wane. In Turkey Kemal Atatürk made a conscious choice for patriotism and rejected pan-Turkism. This point is made clear in a clause of the Republican People's Party program adopted in 1935 which illustrates vividly the relationship between political identity and historiography. "The fatherland is the sacred country within our present political boundaries, where the Turkish nation lives with its ancient and illustrious history, and with its past glories still living in the depths of its soil."

In Iran too there were spectacular archaeological discoveries and decipherments comparable with those of Egypt, though they came later to the Iranians. It was not that the Iranians had, like the Arabic-speaking peoples, lost their identity within Arab Islam. On the contrary, alone among the peoples conquered in the first onrush of Islam, they had retained it. The Persians adopted Islam and the Arabic script, but not the Arabic language. They preserved their own language and a strong sense of separate cultural identity —but it was cultural and not political, or at best only incidentally political. When, a century or two after the Arab conquest, the Persians tried to revive their national historiographic tradition, they found little to work on. The Sasanids were just remembered and their predecessors totally forgotten, and the Persians had to fall back on mythology, which forms the basis of the great national epic of Firdawsī, the *Shāhnāma*, and of all Muslim-Persian historiography on ancient Iran until our own time. Paradoxically, the communal memory retained only two historical names from antiquity. Cyrus, Xerxes, and Artaxerxes were all forgotten. Darius was remembered, in a confused and conflated form, based on three monarchs of that name.[33] But far more important was Alexander, who, as Iskandar, became the hero of a Persian heroic cycle. As so often happens, the foreign conqueror was made into a native, and Alexander was presented in the myth as a Persian prince claiming his own.[34]

[33] See *Encyclopaedia of Islam*, second edition, s.v. "Dārā" (by B. Carra de Vaux and H. Massé).

[34] See *Encyclopaedia of Islam*, second edition, s.vv. "Iskandar" (by W. Montgomery Watt) and "Iskandar nāma" (by A. Abel), where further references are given.

Here there is an obvious parallel with the argument of the English lawyer-historians of the 17th century who refused to see in the Norman Conquest an overthrow or discontinuity, but insisted that William was a lawful claimant to the throne establishing his right.

The revival of interest in antiquity came about through the work of modern Persian historians, novelists, and poets, and was in due course taken over and made state policy under the present dynasty. It serves several purposes: to foster a sense of Persian continuity and national identity on the national soil through the millennia, and to link this with the institution of monarchy as the binding force and the focus of loyalty. And in strengthening the national consciousness it has, at the same time, the effect of weakening the religious one and of making Persians think of themselves first as Persians and only then as Muslims.

Cyrus has been dead for two and a half millennia and was forgotten by his own people though remembered with honor by others. The defenders of Masada too were forgotten by their own people, and remembered only by a renegade who wrote for a foreign audience in a foreign language. Yet both have been recovered, reinterpreted, and given a new role in the modern history of their respective nations.

CHAPTER TWO

MEDIUM AND MESSAGE

The earliest expressions of the collective memory of a community are usually literary. In some parts of Africa the chants sung by the tribes at the annual round-up of the cattle record the history of the tribe for many generations, sometimes extending as far back as three centuries. While the chronology of such recollections is inevitably vague, the points on which they can be checked by some outside evidence—the testimony of some Portuguese or Arab traveller or the like—has shown them to be remarkably accurate in essentials. The Homeric epics of the ancient Greeks, the sagas of the Icelanders, the battle myths of the pre-Islamic Arabs, all serve the same basic purpose. Heroic poetry among a primitive people is intended for recitation aloud and is an invitation to the audience, in the form of a narrative, to admire achievement in conflict by a hero or heroes and thereby to strengthen the morale and the corporate pride of the group. The narrative need not be limited to historical elements, but may draw on mythology, religion, and pure fiction. Normally, it deals with a conflict, a clash between the group, usually exemplified in representative figures—that is to say the heroes of the narrative—and external forces. The latter may be human, of other tribes or peoples, or super-human. It is interesting that in heroic poetry of this kind the essence of achievement lies in the action and in the qualities displayed in the action rather than in the result. The epic hero is not necessarily successful; his career may end in defeat and death, but it serves nonetheless to exalt the honor and courage of the tribe or other entity to which he belongs. Among the Jews, the cult of Masada is new, but among the Serbs, for example, the battle of Kossovo in 1389 is the theme of a whole cycle of heroic literature. Yet Kossovo was a defeat, which established Turkish rule over the Serbs. What mattered, for the poets, was not the outcome, but the heroism of the Serb warriors and their king, and the tales of Kossovo helped to sustain the Serbs during the centuries of their subjection.

Most primitive peoples have heroic narratives of one kind or another which constitute the collective memory of the group, and serve to focus and direct the loyalties of its members and to encourage them in battle and other forms of conflict. This type of functional narrative literature, historical or pseudo-historical, is by no means limited to primitive peoples. There is, however, an important distinction to be made between what might be called primary epic —i.e. that arising spontaneously among a people still living amid or soon after the events which it celebrates—and secondary epic. The latter is something more contrived, more literary, composed at a more advanced state of civilization or a higher social level,

and often by the direction of a patron or even a ruler
seeking to serve some purpose. The classical example
of the contrast can be seen in the difference between
the Greek and Roman epics. The Homeric poems are
spontaneous and primary; the *Aeneid* of Virgil is
self-conscious and derivative. It comes from an imperial not a heroic society; its matter is not living
tradition but literary invention, ascribed to a remote
and largely imaginary past. Its purpose is not merely
to stiffen the morale of the immediate group, but to
promote the new imperial policy of the Roman emperor Augustus. Similar differences, between the contemporary heroic and the contrived literary presentation of the past, may be discerned in the various
narrative passages in the Old Testament. Both types
have continued, with many variants and derivatives,
into modern times, and often skirt or cross the frontier
between memory and invention. In our own day the
development of the mass media, first the theatre, then
the cinema, and, above all, radio and television, has
enormously extended the range and impact of the
popular presentation of the corporate memory.

A second way in which the corporate memory of
the community is preserved and nurtured is through
commemorations—feasts, fasts, and celebrations. Of
the five major festivals of the Jewish year, one, Passover, is explicitly historical, reminding the people
every year of the Exodus, the central event of ancient Jewish history. Two more, the harvest festivals
of Shevuoth and Sukkoth, have been given an his-

torical connotation—the first commemorating the
revelation of the law on Mount Sinai, the second al-
luding to the Exodus from Egypt. The two minor
festivals, Purim and Hanukka, are both explicitly
historical and deal with events which are remembered every year. In addition to these there are numerous lesser historical commemorations, foremost
among them the fast on the ninth day of the month
of Ab, in mourning for the destruction of the temple.
Others include the fast of Gedaliah, lamenting the
death of a wise governor of Judea under Babylonian
rule, and a whole series of other, minor commemorations, either fasts, recalling some misfortune which
befell the Jews, or celebrations of their escape from
some great danger. Even the Sabbath is presented in
the Pentateuch in quasi-historical terms, as a commemoration not only of the creation of the world
but also of the Exodus from Egypt (Leviticus XXIII:
29-43). Virtually the only historical texts of the rabbinical period are lists of commemorative festivals
and fasts. The historical information which they
contain is very meager.

The establishment of such commemorations did
not cease with antiquity but continued through the
Middle Ages as, for example, in the institution of
several local Purim festivals celebrating the escape
of a Jewish community from some impending disas-
ter.[1] Apart from the actual holidays in the calendar

[1] Especially in Egypt. For examples, see Steinschneider, *Geschichtsliteratur*, pp. 97-98; Arabic text ed. Nissim Abraham

devoted to these events, the Jewish liturgy, daily and weekly, contains numerous references to the historically significant past, reminding the practicing Jew, almost with every prayer he utters and every morsel that he consumes, of the major formative events of the community to which he belongs. This is remembered history at its most explicit and most effective.

The Romans too had commemorative festivals which played an important part in their social and public life, the most important being the commemoration of the foundation of the city of Rome, the starting point of their calendar, and of the establishment of the republic by the overthrow of the early monarchy.

Christianity begins with a single sequence of events in history and above all with the central fact of the crucifixion. This is commemorated annually in the Good Friday and Easter festivals with all the ceremonies attached to them, and is also symbolized in the sign of the cross which—unlike the Crescent or the Shield of David[2]—is more than a mere badge or emblem but is a potent evocation of both the central historical fact and the central religious belief of Christianity.

'Anānī, *Megillat Purim Mitsrayim*, Cairo (Samuel Raḥamim), n.d.; Kehana, *Sifrut ha-historia*, ii, pp. 77f.; J. Mann, *The Jews in Egypt and in Palestine under the Fātimid Caliphs*, reprinted New York (Ktav), 1970, i, pp. 26-32; ii, pp. 30-37.

[2] Cf. Gershem Scholem, *The Messianic Idea in Judaism and Other Essays on Jewish Spirituality*, New York (Schocken), 1971, pp. 257ff. (on the star of David).

The other great Christian historical festival is
Christmas. The contrast between Christmas and
Easter is interesting and significant. The one commemorates the birth of Christ, the other his death
and resurrection. It is true that the Easter festival
coincides approximately with the Jewish Passover,
but there is no serious doubt about the historicity of
the crucifixion or the date on which it occurred. The
birth of Christ, on the other hand, is quite a different
matter, and critical scholarship has come to the con-
clusion that the birthdate and even the birthplace of
Christ are uncertain. It was not until comparatively
late that December 25 was formally adopted as
Christ's birthday and celebrated accordingly. There
is little doubt that it represents a Christian adoption
and adaptation of earlier festivals celebrating the
winter solstice, and especially the Roman Saturnalia,
to which was later added the Norse Yule.

Apart from these two major historical festivals
Christianity has many others with a historical basis,
including the innumerable saints' days throughout
the year, each commemorating some historical event,
some religious hero or martyr, many of them with
special local significance. As in Judaism, so in Christianity, ritual and liturgy play an important part in
reviving and reinforcing the corporate recollection of
the remembered past. On the whole the Christian
liturgy is less explicit and less insistent in its reference to history than is the liturgy of the synagogue.
On the other hand, the church more than compen-

sates for this by the pictorial representation of the major events of Christian history. The stained glass windows, paintings, and statuary in the churches serve as a constant reminder to the faithful of the formative and significant events of the Christian past.

Islam as a religion is more overtly historical than either Christianity or Judaism, and its birth is a more explicitly defined sequence of historical events. The founder of Judaism is difficult to name; the founder of Christianity suffered and died on the cross, and his followers remained a persecuted minority for centuries. The founder of Islam became a sovereign in his lifetime, governing a community, administering justice, and commanding armies, and history of the conventional type begins with his own career. Perhaps for this very reason, the major Muslim festivals are not primarily historical. The birthday of the Prophet Muḥammad is, however, celebrated as a minor festival, and the birthdays of numerous local holy men are also commemorated by feasts and fairs in much the same way as the lesser saints of Christendom.[3] The Muslims also seem to have adopted from

[3] See G. E. von Grunebaum, *Muhammadan Festivals,* New York (Henry Schuman), 1951, pp. 67ff. and *Encyclopaedia of Islam,* first edition, s.v. "Mawlid" (by H. Fuchs). The annual pilgrimage to Mecca and Medina, though not a historical commemoration, has some historical associations; it evokes the memory of both Abraham, to whom the Qur'ān attributes both the founding of the sanctuary and the institution of the pilgrimage, and the Prophet Muhammad.

the Jews the practice of compiling historical calendars, known as *taqwīm*, setting forth the anniversaries of major events in the past. The purpose of these is partly to help commemoration, partly to assist in predicting the future.[4]

Until modern times such commemorations were almost exclusively religious; even the foundation of Rome, ostensibly a secular event, was celebrated by priests and with sacrifices. The modern series of commemorative anniversaries seems to have begun with the American July 4 and it is noteworthy that American historians who have tackled this problem critically have been unable to agree on the precise significance of this date. What if anything did happen on the Fourth of July and was it that day anyway? The popular memory, however, is unconcerned with such scholarly niceties. The winning of American independence was a long-drawn-out and complex process, but the popular imagination, as so often, telescoped it into a single dramatic event on a single date suitable for annual celebration.[5] In the same way, a few years later, the storming of the Bastille on July 14 provided the peg on which to hang the annual celebration of that long series of changes and upheavals, the French Revolution.

[4] For some Ottoman *taqwīms*, see Osman Turan, *Istanbul'un fethinden önce yazılmış tarihi takvimler*, Ankara (T.T.K.), 1954.

[5] See for example the discussion in Daniel J. Boorstin, *The Americans: the National Experience*, London (Weidenfeld and Nicolson), 1966, pp. 375ff.

The pattern set by the United States and France
was followed by many other nations, each establishing some national day to provide an occasion for
festivities, speeches, celebrations, and other methods
of restoring and revitalizing the nationalist or revolutionary energy, as the case may be, of the nation
concerned. Even the older nations which have under-
gone the rigors neither of liberation nor of revolution have felt obliged to conform to the pattern and
have chosen, rather arbitrarily, some saint's day or
historical event as a national day. In England, where
the doctrine of the ancient constitution and immemorial liberties of Englishmen precluded the ascribing of a foundation date to either, the monarch's
birthday, officially and permanently fixed in early
June, provides the formal occasion for celebration,
while the popular fancy fastened on Guy Fawkes, a
Catholic conspirator whose failure to blow up Parliament in 1605 is still celebrated with fireworks and
effigies—called guys—every November 5. There are
now more than a hundred embassies and legations in
Washington, each of them with at least one national
celebration to which officials must be invited every
year, and the growing burden of commemoration is
a serious impediment to the conduct of public affairs.

Sometimes the authorities who seek to commemo-
rate some major historical event in which they are
the prime movers are not content with merely setting an anniversary, but seek to establish a new era.[6]

[6] Cf. Paul Couderc, *Le calendrier*, Paris (P.U.F.), 1946.

In most parts of the world it was usual in antiquity to date events from the beginning of a new reign or dynasty. This custom still survives in some parts. The foundation of Rome and the career of Alexander provided the starting points of calendars of more general and extensive usage. Judaism, as a religion which has no specific starting point, had no specific calendar, but used several, finally settling on the present era purporting to date from the creation of the world. Christianity and Islam each envisaged themselves as starting a new era and began new calendars, the one dating from the birth of Christ, the other from the migration of Muḥammad from Mecca to Medina or, more precisely, from the beginning of the Arab year in which that event took place. In more modern times both the French revolutionaries and the Italian fascisti attempted to demonstrate the importance of their achievements and the momentous significance of their advent by starting new calendars. Neither was of long duration.

Another form of remembered history, of more significance in some societies than in others, is surviving custom and law—the living past which is still part of our everyday life. The English Common Law, like the Jewish *Halakha* and the Muslim *Sunna*, is essentially case law, based on old custom as modified by judicial ruling and precedent. In societies governed by this kind of law the role of lawyers—a term which for this purpose includes rabbis and *'ulemā* as well as attorneys at law—is of considerable importance in conserving the memory of the past as embodied in the laws they administer and the institutions through which they administer them.

Finally there is historiography, historical writings written for the express purpose of recording the events of the past for the information and guidance of the present and of the future. These begin in antiquity with inscriptions, in which kings and priests set forth their view of events for the instruction of those who could read—the public relations and propaganda of ancient rulers and patrons. Inscriptions were followed, in ancient and medieval times, by chronicles and biographies of various kinds, usually composed in response to or in expectation of patronage. Those who are in power control to a very large extent the presentation of the past, and seek to make sure that it is presented in such a way as to buttress and legitimize their own authority, and to affirm the rights and merits of the group which they lead.[7] This continuing thread can be traced from ancient inscriptions on rock faces through medieval annals, modern schoolbooks and textbooks, and the official mythology which passes as history in the Soviet Union.

At all stages in the human process there seem to have been small minorities or individuals moved by what we might call scholarly curiosity. They are, however, quite exceptional. Basically, the recovery

[7] Cf. J. H. Plumb, *The Death of the Past*, London (Macmillan), 1969, chapter 1, especially pp. 30ff.

of history is a phenomenon which began in Europe at the time of the Renaissance and remains to the present day primarily a concern and an achievement of West European civilization and of its daughters and disciples in other parts of the world. For some scholars it is this kind of history alone which deserves the name of history—the rest being denoted by such terms as myth, legend, tradition, chronicles, or merely past. The essential and distinctive feature of scholarly research is, or should be, that it is not directed to predetermined results. The historian does not set out to prove a thesis, or select material to establish some point, but follows the evidence where it leads. No human being is free from human failings, among them loyalties and prejudices which may color his perception and presentation of history. The essence of the critical scholarly historian is that he is aware of this fact, and instead of indulging his prejudices seeks to identify and correct them.

The recoverers of history begin of course with what is remembered and transmitted. Unlike their predecessors, however, they are not content merely to repeat and pass on the memories of the past. They seek rather to fill its gaps and correct its errors, and their goals are accuracy and understanding. A frequent result, and sometimes perhaps even a purpose of their efforts, is that by analyzing the past they kill it. The minute and critical examination of treasured memories may reveal them to be false and misleading. Once this exposure becomes generally known, that part of the past loses its power. The scholarly recoverers of the past may therefore exercise a powerful destructive influence. In compensation, they can bring much that is new and enrich the collective memory as well as cleansing it.

Critical history begins with a dissatisfaction with memory and a desire to remedy its deficiencies. But there is more than one kind of dissatisfaction. The critical scholar may be dissatisfied with what remembered history offers him because he feels that it is inaccurate or deficient or misleading. But there are others whose dissatisfaction springs from a different cause. They would rather rewrite history not as it was, or as they have been taught that it was, but as they would prefer it to have been. For historians of this school the purpose of changing the past is not to seek some abstract truth, but to achieve a new vision of the past better suited to their needs in the present and their aspirations for the future. Their aim is to amend, to restate, to replace, or even to recreate the past in a more satisfactory form. Here we may recall two of the main purposes of remembering the past, for communities as for individuals. One is to explain and perhaps to justify the present—a present, some present—on which there may be dispute. Where there are conflicting loyalties or clashing interests, each will have its own version of the past, its own presentation of the salient events. As

Dr. Plumb has remarked, "Warring authorities means warring pasts."[8] It is such situations which lead and have led, from immemorial antiquity, to the invention of the past, that is, to the improvement of memory.

A second use of the past, from very early times, has been to predict and even to control the future. This is manifested in the oracle-bones of ancient China, the omen tablets of Babylon, the messianic tracts of the Jews, Christians, and Muslims, Nostradamus, Old Moore's Almanac, and the Marxist-Leninist classics of modern Communism.[9] They are all equally reliable.

Invention is of several types, and has several functions. Broadly, its aim is to embellish—to correct or remove what is distasteful in the past, and replace it with something more acceptable, more encourag-

[8] Cf. Plumb, p. 40.

[9] Cf. Plumb, pp. 62-64. On Jewish messianism, see G. Scholem, *The Messianic Idea in Judaism*; J. Klausner, *The Messianic Idea in Israel*, translated from the Hebrew by W. F. Stinespring, London (George Allen & Unwin), 1956; Abba Hillel Silver, *A History of Messianic Speculation in Israel*, Boston (Beacon Press), 1959 (first published 1927). On Muslim messianism, the best short accounts are still contained in three articles on the term *Mahdī*: by D. S. Margoliouth in *Hastings Encyclopaedia of Religion and Ethics*; by C. Snouck Hurgronje in his *Verspreide Geschriften*, i, Bonn and Leipzig (Kurt Schroeder), 1923, pp. 147-181, and by D. B. MacDonald in the *Encyclopaedia of Islam*, first edition. See further the articles Djafr (by T. Fahd) in *Encyclopaedia of Islam*, second edition, and Malāḥim (by D. B. MacDonald) in *Encyclopaedia of Islam*, first edition.

ing, and more conducive to the purpose in hand. It may be spontaneous, as in the heroic sagas, romantic, as in a good deal of 19th- and 20th-century writing, or officially sponsored and even imposed.

Much of it is literary, and continues or imitates the tradition of the old heroic poems. The famous Portuguese epic, the Lusiads of Camoens, though derivative and neo-classical in form, deals with contemporary events and presents an idealized version of the great Portuguese discoveries and conquests, in which the poet himself was a proud participant. The events in Palestine in 1929 and in Kashmir in 1947 have been described in Arabic and Pathan war-songs, in the true heroic style; in a different key, the American opening of the West and conquest of the Indian have been similarly celebrated in legend and balladry, in the whole neo-epical and pseudo-epical cycles of cowboy and Indian stories, in song and verse, fiction and film. Through these, as well as through schoolbooks and children's literature, they occupy a place in American corporate self-awareness comparable with the heroic memories of Greece and the imperial consciousness of Rome. Of late there has been some revulsion from the traditional self-congratulatory view of the conquest of the American West, but it still falls far short of the change which took place in the Mexican view of the past, when, as part of their revolution, they began to distinguish between their Hispanic and Indian heritages and to identify themselves more and more with the latter.

The European visitor to the United States and to Mexico cannot but be struck by the contrast between the attitudes of the two to the Indians. While Americans speak, with guilt or otherwise, of "what we did to the Indians," Mexicans, even of pure European descent, speak of "what the Spaniards did to us." The contrast is driven home in the vast historical murals painted by Diego Rivera for the Palacio Nacional in Mexico City.

The romantic movement and its child, the historical novel, have exercised enormous influence in shaping and, all too often, distorting the popular image of the past. The novels of Sir Walter Scott, the pioneer of the art, in themselves illustrate the contrast between remembered and invented history. His novels of 18th-century Scotland reflect a living and authentic memory; his medieval romances are artificial constructs, presented against the background of a past that never was. It was the latter that served as models for his great French successor Alexandre Dumas, and for a host of imitators who set to work to recreate the past as national pride required it to have been. During the 19th and early 20th centuries Jewish, Arabic, Persian, and Turkish historical novelists did much to form the self-image of the new, secular-educated reading public among these peoples, with far-reaching political consequences.

The embellishment or idealization of the past is by no means a romantic or modern innovation, nor is it confined to what are avowedly works of fiction. The past serves a number of purposes, and the art of manipulating it to achieve them goes back to remote antiquity. It is one of the components of mythology; it influences inscriptions and chronicles, monographs and textbooks, and all the other media used to project an image and present a case.

A characteristic example of embellishment is what might be called foundation myth. Most countries and peoples and powers arise from humble origins, and having risen to greatness seek to improve or conceal their undistinguished beginnings and attach themselves to something older and greater. Thus the Romans, rising in power, felt themselves upstarts beside the Greeks, and therefore tried to trace their pedigree from the Trojans. The barbarian peoples of Europe, ruling over the ruins of the Roman Empire, again sought to provide themselves with noble and ancient ancestries, and produced a series of mythical Roman, Greek, or Trojan founders for the various barbarian tribes.[10] Similarly, in Islam, newly converted dynasties in Africa and elsewhere procured themselves remote ancestors of Prophetic, Caliphal,

[10] On medieval European historiographic myths, see R. W. Southern, "Aspects of the European Tradition of Historical Writing: i. The Classical Tradition from Einhard to Geoffrey of Monmouth," in *Transactions of the Royal Historical Society*, vth series, vol. 20, pp. 173ff., and especially pp. 188ff. For Islamic examples, see P. M. Holt, *Studies in the History of the Near East*, London (Cass), 1973, pp. 67ff. and 220ff.; P. Wittek, *The Rise of the Ottoman Empire*, London (Royal Asiatic Society), 1938, chapter 1.

or at the very least Arab origin. The Ottoman sultans tried to link themselves to the Seljuks and thus to earlier Islamic sovereignties, and most of the dynasties of Europe and Asia claimed pedigrees more ancient than critical historiography could justify. Sometimes whole states and nations have tried to modify or transform their origins and identity, often as an expression of inner ideological conflicts. The interaction of the Pharaonic and Arab personalities of Egypt, of the Aztec and Spanish faces of Mexico, are examples. A unique case of changing historical self-image is that of the Christian Empire of Constantinople, whose people began as Greeks pretending to be Romans and ended as Byzantines pretending to be Hellenes.[11]

Even revolutions need some kind of a past, and the official myths of the English, American, French, and Russian revolutions, not to speak of more recent upheavals, are vastly different from the sometimes disagreeable realities uncovered by historians—that is, where historians are permitted to do so without psychiatric treatment. Revolutions also illustrate in a peculiarly vivid way another type of historical invention—the conscious imitation or reenactment of earlier events seen as models. The Jacobin fascination with the Roman republic, the Bolshevik miming of

[11] Cf. Cyril Mango, "Byzantinism and Romantic Hellenism," in *Journal of the Warburg and Courtauld Institutes*, xxxiii (1965), pp. 29-43; Romilly Jenkins, *Byzantium and Byzantinism*, Cincinnati (Univ. of Cincinnati), 1963.

the French Revolution, can be seen both in their actions and still more in their utterances. The same kind of ritual reenactment of the past appears, in a grotesque form, in the restoration of beheading with the axe in Nazi Germany, and of penal mutilation in modern Libya.

Another function of the past is to legitimize authority. In a sense this is the same purpose as embellishment, but more specific in its aims and methods. Examples of this are the rabbinic claims to the inheritance of authority from the elders and prophets and their assertion of the divine origin of the oral law. The consensus of the Muslim *'ulemā* and their attribution of a vast corpus of sayings to the Prophet Muḥammad provides a parallel case. A very striking example of this is the argument at the time of the great struggle in England in the 17th century between the king and parliament, when the anti-monarchists developed the notions of "immemorial custom" and "the ancient constitution" of England. If the king was the source of authority and the fountain of law, then the king could change law at will, and this was not acceptable to the parliamentarians. To circumvent this difficulty, they devised the doctrine of the ancient constitution of Britain and the immemorial custom of the English, their origins lost in antiquity, devised through millennia by the people, and therefore establishing certain rights not subject to change or challenge. Even the Norman Conquest—the forcible overthrow of one regime and the establishment of a new monarchy in its place by conquest—did not baffle the parliamentarian lawyer-historians, who were able to fit this into their scheme of things by presenting William the Conqueror as a legitimate claimant obtaining his heritage in accordance with the ancient constitution.[12]

One method of claiming legitimacy is by attaching one's regime to some earlier and recognized predecessor, which here serves the purpose of providing not merely dignity but also authority. The fake ancestries and fabricated documents that abounded in medieval Europe are good examples of this. So too are the numerous dynasties in the Muslim world who claimed ancestry from the Prophet or from the early heroes of Islam, thereby acquiring a legitimacy in Muslim eyes which they would otherwise have lacked. A religious example is the doctrine of the perpetual orthodoxy of the Maronite church of Lebanon, accomplished by rewriting the earlier history of the sect in order to disguise its heterodox origins and demonstrate that it had always been in communion with Rome.[13]

Sometimes the purpose is accomplished by plain

[12] See J. G. A. Pocock, *The Ancient Constitution and Feudal Law: a Study of English Historical Thought in the Seventeenth Century*, Cambridge (C.U.P.), 1957, p. 53.

[13] See Kamal S. Salibi, *Maronite Historians of Medieval Lebanon*, Beirut (A.U.B.), 1959, especially pp. 137ff.; idem, "The Maronite Church in the Middle Ages and Its Union with Rome," in *Oriens Christianus*, xlii (1958), pp. 92-104.

forgery, as for example in the notorious case of the donations of Constantine, the supposed grant by the Emperor Constantine to the Pope Sylvester and his successors of spiritual supremacy over other patriarchs and bishops and of temporal authority over Rome, Italy, and "the provinces, places, and *civitates* of the western regions." This document was forged some time in the 8th century, to buttress the claims of the papacy, and was first exposed by the humanist scholar Laurentius Valla in 1440. The ensuing controversy lasted until the end of the 18th century, when the case for the defense was finally abandoned. Parallel forgeries in Islam are the letters ascribed to the Prophet, and the so-called Pact of 'Umar, in which the Caliph 'Umar is alleged to have set forth the restrictions imposed on the non-Muslim subjects of the Muslim state.[14]

Nowadays, simple forgery of this kind is rare, though not unknown. The most famous—and successful—forgery of modern times is undoubtedly the so-called "Protocols of the Elders of Zion," which was aptly described by Norman Cohn as a "warrant for genocide," and has successively served the pur-

[14] On historical forgery see W. Ullmann, *A History of Political Thought: the Middle Ages*, London (Penguin), 1965, pp. 80-85, 97-98, and Plumb, pp. 79-80. On the "Pact of 'Umar" see Antoine Fattal, *Le statut légal des non-musulmans en pays d'Islam*, Beirut (Imprimerie Catholique), 1958, pp. 6off.; A. S. Tritton, *The Caliphs and Their Non-Muslim Subjects*, Oxford (O.U.P.), 1930, pp. 5ff.

poses of Tsarist Russia, Nazi Germany, and the less scrupulous Arab governments.[15] More often, and in more sophisticated societies, the desired result is achieved by discreet doctoring of the past. The totalitarian governments of our century have shown themselves particularly adept in this technique.

Sometimes the purpose of the inventors of history is not to legitimize authority but to undermine it— to assert new claims and new arguments, sometimes even a new identity, in conflict with the old order. An obvious example of this is nationalist history— usually of little value to the historian except for the historian of nationalism, but invaluable to him. This arose with the new idea of the nation as the basic political entity. At a time when most of the states of Europe were defined territorially and governed by dynastic monarchies, the new and revolutionary notion was propounded that the nation, defined by language, culture, and origin, constituted the true unit of political identity. From this it followed that any nation which had not expressed its nationhood in

[15] Norman Cohn, *Warrant for Genocide: the Myth of the Jewish World-Conspiracy and the Protocols of the Elders of Zion*, London (Eyre & Spottiswoode), 1967. On the use of the Protocols by Arab writers, see Y. Harkabi, *Arab Attitudes to Israel*, Jerusalem (Israel Universities Press), 1972, p. 229 and index. When the French Foreign Minister Michel Jobert visited Saudi Arabia in January 1974, each of the French journalists permitted to accompany him received as parting gift a package containing the Protocols of the Elders of Zion and an anti-Semitic anthology (*Le Monde*, January 29, 1974).

statehood was somehow deprived; and, correspondingly, that any state not based on a nation was, so to speak, somehow depraved. This led to a massive undermining and redirection of political loyalties, and ultimately to the breakup of the European state system and its reconstitution in different groupings determined by different criteria. The 20th century extended the benefits of nationalism to the rest of the world—and the tale of blood is not yet ended.[16] Nationalist historiography rejects the dynastic past, rejects the old loyalties, rejects even the previous basis of group identity. Nationalist historiography, coinciding with the romantic age, presents a highly colored version of the past, the purpose of which is to encourage these new notions and destroy the old. A Syrian government decree of May 30, 1947 lays down that the purpose of studying and teaching history is "to strengthen the nationalist and patriotic sentiments in the hearts of the people . . . because the knowledge of the nation's past is one of the most important incentives to patriotic behaviour."[17] What could be clearer?

Other examples are reformist history with the more moderate aim of reforming the existing system, and revolutionary historiography with the more ambitious one of destroying and remaking it. Most of

[16] See Elie Kedourie's introduction to his *Nationalism in Asia and Africa*, New York (New American Library), 1970.

[17] Cit. Anwar G. Chejne, "The Use of History . . . ," pp. 392-393.

them seek roots in the past, often in a past con-
structed for the purpose. The 19th-century Russian
scholar T. N. Granovsky was caustic about "the senile
complaints of those who love not the real living
Russia but an ancient ghost, summoned by them
from the grave; and who dishonor themselves by
bowing down before an idol which their own idle
imagination has created."[18] Such idolatry and such
idle imagination are now commonplace in much of
the world.

The myth of the golden age in the past, with the
related assumption of immemorial rights and privileges, is a very widespread one. It was used by the
English parliamentarians to justify their case against
the monarchy, which they rested on the immemorial
custom of the English. Sometimes it took the form
of attributing these customs to the Anglo-Saxons and
thus linking this concept with another related idea,
that of the ancient freedom of the Germanic peoples
in their native forests. This idea won a good deal of
support among German romantics and provided part
of the ideological underpinning of 19th-century German liberalism.

When the nationalist bug was transmitted by Europe to Asians and Africans, similar ideas began to
appear in their nationalist writings. These ideas were
particularly useful in easing the difficult process of

[18] Cit. Leonard Schapiro, *Rationalism and Nationalism in Russian Nineteenth-Century Political Thought*, New Haven and
London (Yale Univ. Press), 1967, pp. 78-79.

borrowing ideas and institutions from an alien and stronger civilization. To have to borrow from others was galling and damaging to national pride. The hurt was much eased, and indeed even transformed into a pleasure, if it could be shown that what was borrowed was not really foreign at all but was something native which the foreigners themselves had borrowed at an earlier date. A rich mythology of the golden age of Muslim civilization, fed partly by European scholarship, partly by oriental fantasy, helped to provide an Islamic origin for almost everything worth borrowing in Europe and thereby to smooth the way for its acceptance.[19]

A more explicitly political form of this process was the myth of ancient freedom, of the English type, but applied to Arabs and to Turks. Thus, in the Arab version, the ancient Arabians in their peninsula had been free and democratic but lost these qualities when they came under the rule of the autocratic Turks. In the Turkish version, the Turks in their native steppes of central Asia had been free and democratic, but lost these qualities when they came under the influence of the authoritarian Muslim Arabs. Both

[19] G. E. von Grunebaum, *Modern Islam*; idem, *Studien zum Kulturbild und Selbstverständnis des Islams*, Zürich and Stuttgart (Artemis), 1969, part ii; W. Cantwell Smith, *Islam in Modern History*, Princeton, N.J. (Princeton Univ. Press), 1957; Walther Braune, *Der islamische Orient zwischen Vergangenheit und Zukunft*, Berne and Munich (Francke), 1960; B. Lewis, *The Middle East and the West*, New York (Harper & Row), 1966 (first published 1964).

are of course absurdly false, yet both are in a sense right, in that both Turks and Arabs arrived as simple primitive peoples and were transformed by something which was neither Turkish nor Arab but the ancient civilization of the Middle East with its millennial autocratic and bureaucratic traditions. It is also somewhat misleading to describe the primitive freedoms of the tribesmen as democratic. Democracy, however one interprets this much misused term, designates a way of organizing authority in the state. It does not apply to nomadic tribal society, where there is no state and very little authority.

A more modern and more sophisticated version of this type of mythology can be seen in some of the writings of the so-called revisionist school in the United States, which look back to a golden age of American virtue and ascribe virtually all the sins and crimes of the world to the present establishment in their country. These writers, with their ruthless disregard of fact and probability alike and their highly ideological motivation, provide an almost exact counterpart to Soviet official historiography, the only difference being that the one is intended to maintain the establishment, the other to replace it. Both are equally ahistorical, in the deepest sense.

When the radical or revolutionary opposition group is finally able to win power, its demands on the past undergo a subtle change. Previously the function of the past was to undermine authority and justify its overthrow. Now it must be made to legitimize authority, that is to say, the newly established authority, which is, however, a revolutionary one. The problem is to justify a successful revolution without at the same time justifying further revolutions against the first one—or to justify an existing authority without at the same time justifying a restoration of that which it has just overthrown. The political instability and historiographic chaos of many of the countries of Asia, Africa, and Latin America illustrate the difficulty of this problem. Probably the only solution to it is that discovered and practiced by the Soviet Union—complete state control of the means of production, distribution, and exchange of historical knowledge and writing.

Short of the Soviet method of state-imposed control and direction, there are various ways in which the invention of history can be encouraged and directed. One is patronage, another popular success, another official fraud—when practiced on behalf of a church known as pious fraud—another ideology. But the most effective by far is force. This not only means that the past has to be rewritten to accord with the requirements of the present; it further means that every time there is a change in the present through the triumph of one faction over another, or even a change of policy within the ruling faction, the past must again be rewritten to accord with the requirements of the new present. It is not for nothing that a Soviet historian once remarked that the most difficult of a historian's tasks is to predict the past.

CHAPTER THREE

AS IT SHOULD HAVE BEEN

"Tell it like it was," runs a common American phrase, echoing, no doubt unconsciously, Leopold von Ranke's famous injunction to write history "wie es eigentlich gewesen"—how it really was.[1] But this is neither as simple nor as easy as it sounds. What happened, what we recall, what we recover, what we relate, are often sadly different, and the answers to our questions may be both difficult to seek and painful to find. The temptation is often overwhelmingly strong to tell it, not as it really was, but as we would wish it to have been. In what has gone before I have endeavored to define and to illustrate the three different types of historical material offered to readers of history—remembered, recovered, and invented history. I should like now to consider a number of specific examples drawn principally from the history of the Muslim world.

My first example is the recovery of the lost glories of Muslim Spain. In 1492, with the conquest of Granada, the last stronghold of the Muslims in the Iberian peninsula, where they had reigned for eight

---

[1] L. Ranke, *Geschichte der romanischen und germanischen Voelker 1495-1535*. Berlin (von Dunker and Humblot), 1874, p. vii. Cf. the observations of G. J. Renier on what Ranke meant and did not mean by this phrase; Renier, *History: Its Purpose and Method*, London (George Allen & Unwin), 1950, p. 130.

hundred years, was overcome, and in the same year
an edict by the Catholic monarchs decreed the ex-
pulsion of "Moors and Jews" from all the lands of
the Spanish crowns. Many Spanish Muslims fled to
North Africa, a few to the Middle East, and for a
while the memory and nostalgia of the lost lands of
Andalus lingered on. In the early 17th century a
Moroccan historian called al-Maqqarī wrote a vast
encyclopaedic work on the history and literature of
Muslim Spain from the beginning to the end. Thereafter this chapter in Muslim history, this lost land
where Muslims had once ruled, were substantially
forgotten in the Muslim world. Some memories lingered on in North Africa among the descendants of
the exiles; in the East the once glorious civilization
of Muslim Spain faded into oblivion.

The recovery of this chapter in Muslim history
was entirely the work of Europeans, some of them
Spanish, others of various European nationalities. Al-
Maqqarī's long hymn to the glory of Andalus was
first printed in London in 1840, in an incomplete
English translation by the Spanish scholar Pascual
de Gayangos.[2] The Arabic text first saw the light of

[2] Pascual de Gayangos, *The History of the Mohammedan
Dynasties in Spain*, London (Oriental Translation Fund), 1840-
1843. On the Spanish Arabists of the 19th century see Manuela
Manzanares de Cirre, *Arabistas españoles del siglo XIX*, Madrid
(Instituto hispano-arabe de cultura), 1972. On Arabic studies in
Europe in general, see Johann Fück, *Die arabischen Studien in
Europa bis den Anfang des 20 Jahrhunderts*, Leipzig (Otto
Harrassowitz), 1955.

day in Leiden, Holland, where an edition of the first part was published between 1855 and 1861, jointly edited by the Dutchman Dozy, the Englishman Wright, the Frenchman Dugat, and the German Krehl.

The history of Moorish Spain attracted a great deal of attention in Europe in the early 19th century, where a cult of Spain formed an important component of the romantic movement. Washington Irving in particular wrote about the sunset glories of the Alhambra and the vanished greatness of Muslim Spain. A French historian, Louis Viardot, wrote a book called *Essai sur l'histoire des arabes et des maures d'Espagne*, published in Paris in two volumes in 1833. It was a popularizing work of no great scholarly merit, but it had a considerable impact in the East. The rediscovery by the Muslims of the Spanish chapter in their past can be dated with precision from the publication, in Istanbul, in 1863-1864, of a Turkish translation of this book. An Arabic translation of Chateaubriand's romantic tale of Moorish Spain, *The Last of the Abencerages*, appeared in Algiers in 1864.[3] The Turkish version of Viardot was reprinted in four volumes in 1886-1887, just about the time when Muslim interest in Andalus was be-

[3] Listed in H. Pérès, "Le roman, le conte et la nouvelle dans la litterature arabe moderne," in *Annales de l'Institut d'Études Orientales* (Algiers), iii (1937), p. 27. Further translations and adaptations of the same story were published in 1909, 1918, 1922, and 1925.

coming more extensive. This interest was nourished
from two sources. One, and the more important, was
the attendance by Muslims for the first time at international congresses of Orientalists, where they made
the acquaintance of European Oriental scholarship
and in particular the work done by European scholars on the history of Spain under Muslim rule. This
led to the second source—the decision of the Ottoman
sultan Abdulhamīd II in 1886 to send emissaries to
Spain in search of Arabic manuscripts.

These were the first of a long series of pilgrims
from Turkey, Egypt, and other Muslim countries
and even from faraway India to visit the great sites
and monuments of the Spanish Muslim past. Numerous works were translated and then written in Arabic, Turkish, and other languages of Islam on Spanish Muslim history, and a whole romantic literature
of plays and novels appeared in these languages, with
their setting in a semi-mythical Cordova, seen as a
golden age.[4]

It is not difficult to understand the attraction of
Andalus for Muslims. This was a time when the
Muslim world, from Morocco to Indonesia, was in
retreat and being subjected more and more to the

---

[4] See further Bernard Lewis, *Islam in History: Ideas, Men and
Events in the Middle East*, London (Alcove), 1973, chapters
1, 9, and 10; Aziz Ahmad, "Islam d'Espagne et Inde musulmane
moderne," in *Études d'orientalisme dédiées à la mémoire de
Lévi-Provençal*, ii, Paris (Maisonneuve & Larose), 1962, pp. 461-
470; Henri Pérès, *L'Espagne vue par les voyageurs musulmans de
1610 à 1930*, Paris (Adrien-Maisonneuve), 1937.

overwhelming strength of Christendom, by the advance of Europe from both ends—the Portuguese, then the Spaniards, the French, the Dutch, and the English from Western Europe and the Russians from Eastern Europe, advancing first on the extremities and then into the very heartlands of Islam. The cult of Andalus met a deep emotional need among Muslim intellectuals. At a time when, thanks to the European education they were receiving, they were becoming painfully aware of their own weakness and backwardness, they could find sustenance and comfort in the memory of a great, rich, civilized, and powerful Muslim state in Europe, a state which, as they imagined, had been the guide and leader of European civilization. In the time of their own decline and defeat, they could find melancholy parallels in the sunset splendors of the Alhambra. The glories of Andalus became a favorite theme of the poets and novelists of nostalgia. The real and still more the imagined achievements of Spanish-Arab civilization provided proof-texts for the romantic and the apologetic school of Islamic historiography which was growing up in answer to the devastating impact of the West and the feelings of inferiority which it engendered.

The fact that the history and civilization of Muslim Spain were made known to them entirely thanks to the efforts of Western scholars was in itself a hard pill to swallow. This fact is therefore generally concealed, and some Muslim "historians" have gone so far as to allege that this glorious chapter in Muslim history and the immense Muslim contribution to European civilization through Spain were deliberately hidden from sight by malicious and prejudiced European historians out of hostility to Islam. It was a poor return from the inventors of history to the discoverers who provided them with their raw material.

For Muslim inventors of Spanish-Arab history Spanish Islam was the fountainhead of the arts and sciences—the source from which Europe drew all that is best and most original in its civilization. This doctrine, which has a sufficient element of truth in it to lend it credibility, served a double purpose: on the one hand, of providing solace for the hurt pride of conquered Muslim peoples; on the other, of making borrowings from Europe more acceptable by ascribing to them an ultimate Arab Islamic origin.

One of the qualities which these historians particularly delighted in ascribing to Spanish Islam was the virtue of tolerance. The myth of Spanish Islamic tolerance in itself provides an interesting example of the dangers and ambiguities of historiography. First there is the question of what precisely the word means. For some, tolerance means the absence of persecution—rather as, at the present time, Soviet spokesmen indignantly disclaim anti-Semitism, because they do not send Jews to gas chambers. For others, tolerance means the absence of discrimination—a situation in which all enjoy equal rights and privileges irrespective of race, creed, or origin. If tolerance means the absence of persecution then, on the whole, Spanish Islam was a tolerant society and it is not surprising that the European liberal historians of the early 19th century, contrasting it with the practice of medieval Europe or even of the Europe of their own day, were able in good faith to describe it as tolerant. If however tolerance means the absence of discrimination, then Spanish Islam never was nor pretended nor claimed to be tolerant. Indeed, tolerance in this sense of the word would have been regarded by Muslim jurists and historians alike not as a virtue but as a dereliction of duty, a sin against the holy law of Islam, which prescribes the superiority of the true believers, while at the same time assigning a tolerated but inferior place to others.

The myth of Spanish Islamic tolerance was fostered particularly by Jewish scholars, who used it as a stick with which to beat their Christian neighbors.[5] In our own time it has been taken up by Muslim scholars who use it for their own somewhat different purposes. The ultimate in absurdity comes from a distinguished Muslim scholar, a Pakistani, who, in a book published in 1951, speaking of the non-Muslim subjects of the Muslim state in classical times, remarks: "They have complete protection of life, creed, and honor; neither any economic nor any legal liability shall be imposed on them. They have complete

[5] See Lewis, *Islam in History*, pp. 123ff.

equality of opportunity and equality before law."[6]

This statement is false in almost every particular. Yet its author, whom I knew personally, was both a learned and an honest man and firmly believed a statement which was in flagrant contradiction with the evidence of history, the prescriptions of law, and the facts which he saw about him in his everyday life. It is a striking testimonial to the power of historical invention and an example of a myth particularly persistent in the present time, when it serves a useful and obvious political purpose.

Sometimes the material provided by the recoverers of history presents some problems of acceptance. The great north African Arab historian Ibn Khaldūn (1332-1406) was by common consent the greatest and most original of all historical thinkers who flourished in Islam and indeed one of the greatest historians who ever lived. It is a curious fact that his work, indeed his name, were virtually forgotten among the Arabs. He survived and was read among the Turks,

[6] Khalifa Abdul Hakim, *Islam and Communism*, Lahore (Institute of Islamic Culture), 2nd edition, 1953, pp. 157-158. For more dispassionate assessments of Muslim tolerance see Rudi Paret, "Toleranz und Intoleranz im Islam," in *Saeculum*, XXI (1970), pp. 344-365; Francesco Gabrieli, *Arabeschi e studi islamici*, Naples (Guida), 1973, chapter 2 (La tolleranza nell'Islam), pp. 23-36; Tilman Nagel, Gerd-R. Puin, Christa-U. Spuler, Werner Schmucker, and Albrecht Noth, *Studien zum Minderheitenproblem in Islam*, Bonn (Selbstverlag des Orientalischen Seminars der Universität), 1973; *Encyclopaedia of Islam*, second edition, s.v. "Dhimma" (by Claude Cahen), and the works by Tritton and Fattal cited above.

and it was probably from a Turkish source that European scholars first heard about him. The publication of Ibn Khaldūn's major historical work, the *Muqaddima* or *Prolegomena*, was the work of a French scholar, Etienne Quatremère; its translation into French the work of another European scholar, the Irishman De Slane, and it was almost entirely the work of European historians, sociologists, and others that led to the appreciation and evaluation of Ibn Khaldūn and to his taking his rightful place in the intellectual history of mankind. It was only at a comparatively late stage that the Arabs themselves became aware of their greatest historian—and awareness brought some problems. Ibn Khaldūn, like all truly great historians, is often critical of his own people, and has some hard words to say about the Arabs and their role in history. The Egyptian philosopher Ahmad Fu'ād al-Ahwānī went so far as to say that Orientalists had accepted Ibn Khaldūn and made much of him only because of his attacks on Arabism and not because of his merits as an historian.[7] Indeed, for a while, the works of Ibn Khaldūn were banned in the republic of Iraq because of his critical comment on the Arabs.

The decline of Arab civilization in the Middle Ages and the falling of the Arabs under the domination of alien peoples has formed the subject of much agonized discussion and soul-searching among Arab

[7] Ahmad Fu'ād al-Ahwānī, *Al-Qawmiyya al-'arabiyya*, Cairo, 1960, p. 98.

historians of the present time. It is only very recently
that the problem has begun to bother them, or indeed
that they have been aware of its existence. Muslim
historians were not accustomed to think in ethnic
terms, and the passing of the leadership of Islam
from the Arabs to Persians, Turks, and others did
not strike Muslim historians as significant or worthy
of special note. Only a very few, among them Ibn
Khaldūn, even show any awareness of this process,
and Ibn Khaldūn regards it as a sign of God's provi-
dential concern for the welfare of the Muslim community that when one race falls into decline and
decay He brings forth another and fresher one to
take over the leadership. It is in these terms that he
presents the decline of the Arabs and the rise of
Turkish supremacy.[8]

Until the very last phase of Ottoman rule in the
Middle East, the Arabs did not see themselves as an
Arab nation subject to a Turkish nation in a Turkish
empire, but saw all of them as fellow Muslims in the
last of the great universal Muslim states, ruled over
by the Muslim sultans. It is only since the fall of the
Ottoman Empire and the rise of Arab national states
and of Arab nationalism that nationalist historians
have begun, as so often, to see history backwards and
write it upside down. The fact of Arab decline, of
which contemporaries were happily unaware, is
clear enough in retrospect and cannot be concealed.

[8] Ibn Khaldūn, *Kitāb al-'Ibar*, v, Cairo, 1867, p. 371; English
translation in B. Lewis, *Islam*, i, pp. 97-99.

It must therefore be explained, and some cause, some villain, found other than the Arabs themselves. The answer of most historians was to blame the Turks and the Mongols, seeing in both the destroyers and subjugators of the great civilization of medieval Islam.[9]

Certainly the coming of the Turks and still more of the Mongols brought great changes to the Islamic civilization of the Middle East, changes comparable in their way with those of the migrations of peoples that accompanied and followed the fall of the Roman Empire. But to ascribe all the ills of the Middle East to Mongol destruction and Turkish misrule is an absurdity. Here again, I may quote a perhaps somewhat grotesque example cited by a Swiss journalist from a high Syrian government official. "If the Mongols had not burnt the libraries of Baghdad in the thirteenth century, we Arabs would have had so much science, that we would long since have invented the atomic bomb. The plundering of Baghdad put us back by centuries."[10] Serious Arab historians would perhaps not go quite as far as the unnamed

[9] For protests against these views, common in school textbooks, see 'Abd al-Karīm Gharā'iba, *Al-'Arab wa'l-Atrāk*, Damascus (Damascus University Press), 1381/1961; Abdallah Laroui, *L'idéologie arabe contemporaine*, Paris (Maspéro), 1970, pp. 22-25; Halil Inalcik, "Some Remarks on the Study of History in Islamic Countries," in *Middle East Journal*, vi (1953), pp. 551-555.

[10] Arnold Hottinger, "Patriotismus und Nationalismus bei den Arabern," in *Neue Zürcher Zeitung*, May 12, 1957. Cit. B. Lewis, *Islam in History*, p. 179.

"high Syrian government official" but there can be little doubt that his remarks accurately represent the general feeling.

The Turks and the Mongols of course have their own versions of history in which the role they play is quite a different one—that of saving a collapsing society, defending it from its external attackers, and launching it on a new path of creative activity.

One of the particular merits claimed by the Turks in Islam is that of having saved the Islamic world from the Crusaders. For this claim they have substantial justification in that the armies and rulers who met the assault of the Crusaders, held them, and finally ejected them, were overwhelmingly Turkish. The Turkishness of the Muslim defense and counterattack is not, however, very much in evidence in the most recent Arab discussions of the Crusades.

The whole attitude of Muslim historiography to the Crusades is in itself an interesting topic. In modern times the Crusades have been variously presented by Muslim historians—as an attack by aggressive, fanatical Christians on an inoffensive Muslim world, as an imperialist invasion and exploitation by Europeans trying to dominate and exploit the Arabs, and, latterly, as a sort of prefigurement of the Balfour Declaration and of Israel—an attempt to create an alien enclave, sustained from the West, in the heart of the Arab world. Curiously enough, Muslim historians at the time of the Crusades—and they are many and voluminous—did not see the Crusades in any of these forms. Indeed, strange as it may seem, they did not see the Crusades at all. While Christian Europe was acutely aware of the great struggle between Islam and Christendom for the control of the Holy Land and the holy places, contemporary Muslims saw no such thing. It is noteworthy that in the immense Muslim historiography of the period of the Crusades, the words "Crusade" and "Crusader" never occur. There appear to have been no Arabic terms for them until they were required much later by Christian Arab writers, and it was not until modern times that they passed into general use in Arabic. Contemporary Muslim historians speak of the Crusaders either as the Franks or as the Infidels, and do not make any distinction between them and the other barbarian and infidel invaders by whom the world of Islam was beset at one point or another, at one place or another in the course of medieval centuries.[11] The arrival of the Crusaders in Palestine and the loss of Jerusalem seems to have meant no more to contemporaries than the loss of any other province or any other provincial city. It was only under the influence and following the example of the Crusaders themselves that the Muslims began to attach importance to this and that the reconquest of Jerusalem by Saladin was celebrated as a great Muslim vic-

[11] See *Encyclopaedia of Islam*, second edition, s.v. "Crusades" (by Claude Cahen); F. Gabrieli, "The Arabic Historiography of the Crusades," in Bernard Lewis and P. M. Holt (editors), *Historians of the Middle East*, London (O.U.P.), pp. 98-107.

tory. But no sooner had they recovered Jerusalem than they lost interest in it again and were even prepared, in the pact concluded between the sultan al-Malik al-Kāmil and the emperor Frederick II in 1229, to cede it back to the Christians, since they wanted it so much.

After the final defeat and withdrawal of the Crusaders the whole affair was forgotten and it was only in modern times, and once again drawing from European sources, that Muslim interest revived. It began with popular historiography and romantic novels and then enjoyed a tremendous development during the last few years, when Muslim historians have tried to see in the wars of the Crusades, and more particularly in the rise and fall of the Crusader principalities, parallels to the events of our own time.[12] Some Arab historians have pursued the theme of the Crusaders back into Europe, and tried to relate it directly to the Jewish question. Thus, in a paper by the professor of medieval history in Cairo University, we find these remarks:

"The hatred felt by various peoples of earth throughout history for Jews was not due to their belief but their actions [and] behavior, and attitude towards the peoples among whom they settled. It is an unchangeable behavior, always based on exploita-

[12] See Emanuel Sivan, "Modern Arab Historiography of the Crusades," in *Asian and African Studies*, viii (1972), pp. 109-149. To the historians studied by Dr. Sivan, one might add the Arabic historical novelists, and the pioneer among them, Jurji Zaydān, whose novel *Saladin and the Assassins* appeared in about 1909.

tion, ingratitude, and evil-doing in return for kindness. . . . Kings, princes, knights, bishops, and laymen of Europe found themselves before groups of Jews living amongst them and heeding neither ethics nor conscience, becoming richer and richer while they themselves became poorer and poorer. The Jews ruthlessly sucked their blood and usurped their properties. This alone was the main cause of the hatred . . . the feeling of exasperation and indignation at a group characterized by ruthlessness and harmfulness. . . . In Germany, the biggest wave of persecution of Jews in the Middle Ages was connected with the Crusades. It was the Jews themselves who adopted a hostile attitude, thinking that the crusades would impede their financial activities. This was not in the West alone, but in the East as well. At the same time the princess [sic] and knights of the first crusade felt it perilous to leave their country for the East, leaving behind cliques of Jews who ruthlessly exploited them. The knights and princes may have been burdened by huge financial responsibilities as a result of the crusades, at the time when they felt that there was no way out of their debts to the Jews except by getting rid of the Jews themselves. Mainz, and other towns of the Rhine basin, witnessed wide-scale massacres in 1096, in which large numbers of Jews were killed."[13]

[13] Sa'id Abdel Fattah Ashour, "Jews in the Middle Ages, Comparative Study of East and West," in Al-Azhar, *The Fourth Conference of the Academy of Islamic Research, September 1968,* Cairo (Govt. Printing Office), 1970, pp. 497-499.

This is fairly typical of writing on Jews in Arabic. It should, however, be added that few reputable academic historians in Arab countries would descend to this level.[14] Few indeed have shown much interest in Jewish history. They have been far more concerned with the Crusaders themselves, and with the parallels they offer.

The lesson to be drawn and the comfort to be derived are obvious. The Crusaders came like Zionists across the sea, settled, and with the help of the European powers set up an independent state in Palestine. For some time it managed to hold its own and inflict defeat after defeat upon the Muslims, but gradually it weakened and in the course of time the Muslims were able to muster the necessary strength to drive the Crusaders finally into the sea.

The moral is obvious—that it may take a century, it may take two, but sooner or later Israel will go the same way. The Crusaders were proto-Zionists, the Zionists are modern Crusaders; both are equivalent to one another. There are, of course, some difficulties in the ways of this interpretation, not least being that the heroes of the counter-crusade were without exception non-Arabs. Saladin and his dynasty were Kurdish, the rest were all Turks; but this can be dealt

[14] On the other hand, "specialists" on Jewish matters go even further, making extensive use, among others, of the blood libel and of the Protocols of the Elders of Zion. For an example of the first, by an Egyptian professor of Hebrew, see Ḥasan Ẓāẓā, as interviewed in *Ākhir Sāʿa*, November 14, 1973. On the Protocols, see p. 64 note 15, above.

with by disregarding it, by misrepresenting it, or, for the more conscientious, by fabricating Arab genealogies. Naturally there is a corresponding interest in the Crusades in Israel, where Israeli historians have looked with anxious concern at their predecessors who set up a state in that area surrounded by a hostile world of Islam and suffered erosion and final extinction. Where Arab historians seek resemblances, the Israeli historians seek differences, and neither have any difficulty in finding what they seek.

Probably the outstanding example in our time of the inventive and purposive use of historiography is the writing of colonial, post-colonial, and finally precolonial history. By the 19th century the greater part of Asia and Africa had come under the domination of four great imperial powers, Britain, France, Holland, and Russia, and of three lesser ones, Portugal, Belgium, and Italy. In the Far East, China and Japan, in the Middle East, Turkey and Persia, remained independent, but with few exceptions the rest of Asia and Africa passed under imperial rule. In all the European empires a considerable effort was made by scholars to study the history, languages, cultures, and antiquities of the peoples over whom they ruled. The accusation is often made that Orientalists were the servants of imperialism and that their researches and writings were designed to serve imperial needs. There is some color in this accusation, in that empire and still more trade provided the opportunity and the means for European scholars to study oriental texts, documents, and archives. As an assessment, however, of either the attitude or the achievement of the great European orientalists the accusation is grotesquely false. Few of them were in any way servants or employees of imperial or commercial interests; many were actively critical of imperial rule and showed greater sympathy with their subjects than with their compatriots.

There were, however, some whose writing of history, consciously or otherwise, did reveal a certain purpose. This is clearer in the earlier, more confident, stage of empire, before the rulers were weakened by feelings of guilt and doubt. This attitude is expressed with devastating clarity in Sir Henry Elliot's preface, dated 1849, to the work which he and John Dowson edited, *The History of India as Told by Its Own Historians*, eight volumes of English translations of the Persian and Arabic sources for the history of Muslim India:

"Though the intrinsic value of these works may be small, they will still yield much that is worth observation to anyone who will attentively examine them. . . . They will make our native subjects more sensible to the immense advantages accruing to them under the mildness and equity of our rule. If instruction were sought for from them, we should be spared the rash declarations respecting Muhammedan India, which are frequently made by persons not otherwise ignorant. . . . We should no longer hear bombastic Baboos, enjoying under our Government the

highest degree of personal liberty, and many more
political privileges than were ever conceded to a
conquered nation, rant about patriotism and the deg-
radation of their present position. If they would
dive into any of the volumes mentioned herein, it
would take these young Brutuses and Phocians a
very short time to learn, that, in the days of that
dark period for whose return they sigh, even the bare
utterance of their ridiculous fantasies would have
been attended, not with silence and contempt, but
with the severer discipline of molten lead or impale-
ment. . . . We shall find that a perusal of these books
will convey many a useful lesson, calculated to foster
in us a love and admiration of our country and its
venerable institutions . . . these considerations . . .
will serve to dissipate the gorgeous illusions which
are commonly entertained regarding the dynasties
which have passed, and show him that—notwithstanding a civil policy and an ungenial climate,
which forbid our making this country a permanent
home, and deriving personal gratification or profit
from its advancement—notwithstanding the many
defects necessarily inherent in a system of foreign
administration, in which language, colour, religion,
customs and laws preclude all natural sympathy between sovereign and subject—we have already, within half a century of our dominion, done more for
the substantial benefit of the people, than our predecessors, in the country of their own adoption, were
able to accomplish in more than ten times that pe-

riod; and, drawing auguries from the past, he would derive hope for the future, that, inspired by the success which has hitherto attended our endeavours, we shall follow them up by continuous efforts to fulfil our high destiny as the Rulers of India."[15]

Similar preoccupations are revealed in a paper by a Soviet scholar on "The State Archives of XIX Century Feudal Khiva." Drawing a somber picture of the state of utter misery and tyranny which preceded the Russian conquest, the author lets slip the interesting remark that "the archive completely destroys the myth about the alleged earthly paradise for the peasants of Khiva"—thereby incidentally revealing first, the existence of such a myth, and second, the Soviet desire to destroy it.[16] The same spirit can be discerned, though rarely as explicitly expressed as by Sir Henry Elliot, in French writings on North Africa and in both Tsarist and Soviet Russian writings on the Caucasus and Central Asia. The purpose is always the same—to blacken the regimes which existed before the coming of empire and to depict their rule as barbarous and tyrannical, thereby justifying the conquest and the maintenance of imperial rule.

[15] *Bibliographical Index to the Historians of Muhammedan India*, i, Calcutta 1849, Preface, xx-xxx, cit. P. Hardy, *Historians of Medieval India: Studies in Indo-Muslim Historical Writing*, London (Luzac), 1960, pp. 8-9.

[16] M. Yuldashev, "The State Archives of XIX Century Feudal Khiva," in *Papers Presented by the Soviet Delegation at the XXIII International Congress of Orientalists*, Moscow (Akademiya Nauk), 1954, pp. 221ff., especially p. 224.

This kind of history was taught to the subjects as well as to the rulers in the empire and provided the intellectual pabulum of native as well as imperial officials. It served the double purpose of discouraging any tendency among the natives to self-assertion and also of sustaining the morale of the rulers in carrying out tasks which they might otherwise have doubted their right to perform.

The questioning of this kind of historiography began principally among the scholars of the imperial nations themselves. It was English historians who tried to achieve a more accurate understanding of the history of pre-British India. It was French historians who challenged and criticized the official myths about the barbarism and backwardness from which the French had rescued North Africa. It was Russian historians, in the brief interlude of liberty after the Soviet Revolution, who challenged the official doctrines of Tsarist paternalism and tried, by empathy, to understand the history and culture of the subject peoples of the Russian Empire contemptuously lumped together under the heading of Tatar. In all these countries, such scholars found eager native disciples willing to take up and carry on their work, and there can be little doubt that, however we may assess their contribution as historians to imperialism, we cannot deny their immense contribution to the rise of nationalism, for which they provided—by scholarly recovery—a very large part of the intellectual material.

But for nationalists, of course, the recovered material was insufficient. More was needed, and when
the British, French, and Dutch finally packed their
bags and departed, new tasks awaited the historians
of the countries which they had left. Today only two
of the European empires survive—the very first to
begin the process, the Russians from Eastern Europe
and the Portuguese from the west. The Russians have
retained their Asian territories, the Portuguese their
African territories, and both still maintain the old
style of imperial rule.[17] For a parallel to Sir Henry
Elliot's contrast of Indian barbarism saved by British
enlightenment, one must turn to modern Soviet historiography and its presentation of the Russian conquest of trans-Caucasia and Central Asia. Communist
government and Marxist doctrine have not prevented
the Great Russians from adopting an extremely nationalist stance in their historiography. In dealing
with the expansion of Tsarist Russia into Asia and
elsewhere, the "progressive" role of Soviet government is reflected back into the past, so that any Russian advance was objectively progressive in that it
initiated the conquered society into a higher state
of development. No such merit is of course allowed
in British, French, or other West European imperial
rule. Russian historians are also ferociously attached
to the antiquity and preeminence of the Slavs, and

[17] Since these words were written a new regime in Portugal
has taken the first steps towards the ending of colonial rule in
Africa. There is no change in Russia.

particularly of their own branch. The theory, at one time generally accepted, of the Viking origin of the first Russian state in Kiev, is vehemently and unanimously rejected by Soviet historians and is seen as an intolerable affront.[18] Here again, an example of the grotesque may be given—in the claim by the Soviet historian Yevgeni Alexandrovitch Belayev that in the medieval Byzantine Empire the toiling masses looked to the wandering Slavic tribes as their allies and liberators.[19] It would be difficult to imagine a more preposterous assertion.

It was in Russia that the de-colonization of historiography—the liberation of the past—first began. The fall of tsardom, the new revolutionary thinking, gave rise to a new approach to the history of the subject peoples of the Russian Empire and of the history of their relationship with the Russian state. The languages, literatures, and monuments of these people were carefully studied. Not only that, but national and religious leaders who had resisted the Russians were exhumed and acclaimed as national heroes—not only in historiography but even in drama, opera, and fiction. The Muslim peoples of Asiatic Russia who, like those of North Africa, had been taught that they were an ethnic dust of broken

[18] See for example B. A. Rybakov, *"La formation de la Russie de Kiev,"* *Rapports de la délégation soviétique au Xe congrès international des sciences historiques à Rome*, Moscow (Akademiya Nauk), 1955.

[19] E. A. Belyaev, *Arabs, Islam and the Arab Caliphate in the Early Middle Ages*, New York (Praeger), 1969, p. 9.

tribes awaiting the civilizing mission of their imperial masters, now learned that, on the contrary, they were the remnants of a great civilization with its own glorious achievements in the past, upon which they could build their national pride and national self-respect.

In Russia the process was halted and reversed. The authority of the central government was reasserted over the dependent territories, and a succession of local heroes who had enjoyed a brief revival as leaders of national liberation movements against imperialism were suddenly demoted to feudal reactionaries resisting the objectively progressive advance of Russia. The national heroes in question, who had been dead for some time, were no doubt untroubled by this transformation, but the historians who had presented them in this light suffered some personal inconvenience as a result of this change of line. Thereafter, anything remotely savoring of national or religious ideology among any of the subject peoples of the Russian Empire was strictly prohibited, and the dogma was maintained, in terms which Sir Henry Elliot would have understood perfectly, that the Russians, even the Tsarist Russians, and still more the Soviet Russians, had rescued these peoples from barbarism and established a better regime than they could ever hope to do themselves.[20] In the same spirit,

[20] See Vincent Monteil, "Essai sur l'Islam en U.R.S.S.," in *Revue des études islamiques*, xx (1952), pp. 5-146; xxi (1953), pp. 1-37; Charles Warren Hostler, *Turkism and the Soviets*, Lon-

Soviet historians explain how pre-colonial Central Asia was explored by a succession of British and Russian officers—the former spies and agents of imperialism, the latter engaged in scholarly and scientific research. When in fact the Russians acquired Central Asia (the word "conquest" is usually avoided), they conferred a double boon on its people— by saving them from the horrors of British imperialism as practiced in India, and by bringing them under the benign guidance of the Great Russian people. Soviet historians might—but do not—add that the Russians, by preempting a British conquest, saved these peoples from the burdens and hazards of democracy and independence borne by Britain's former imperial subjects, and instead kept them safe and sound in the protective bosom of the Soviet family.[21]

---

don (George Allen & Unwin), 1957; Olaf Caroe, *Soviet Empire: the Turks of Central Asia and Stalinism*, London (Macmillan), 1953.

[21] See for example N. A. Khalfin, *Politika Rossii v Sredney Azii (1857-1868)*, Moscow (Izdatelstvo Vostočnoy Literatury), 1960 (condensed English translation by Hubert Evans, *Russia's Policy in Central Asia 1857-68*, London [Central Asian Research Centre], 1964); idem, *Prisoyedinenye Sredney Azii k Rossii (60-90e godi XIX v.)*, Moscow (Nauk), 1965, p. 421, comparing the frank and open Russian visitors to British India with the furtive journeyings and secret plots of a much larger number of British spies, saboteurs, and provocateurs in Russian Central Asia; I. S. Braginsky, S. Radžabov, and V. A. Romodin, "K Voprosom o značinenye prisoyedinenya Sredney Azii k Rossii," in *Voprosi Istorii*, no. 8, 1953. See further *Central Asian Review*, vi (1958), pp. 386-407, and xiv (1966), pp. 350-351.

In the former British, French, and Dutch colonies there was no such reversal, and the process of decolonizing the past went on unabated.[22] The present was saved—their efforts had accomplished that; the future was assured—their ideologies promised them that. There remained the task of rescuing the past from imperialist control. The history that had served the imperialist rulers and their native helpers would not do, was not fitting for the people of independent and sovereign states. To meet the new need a new historiography was devised and teams of historians, or at any rate of teachers and writers of history, were deployed to conquer and liberate the past.

Some of the work they accomplished was of great value. It is perfectly natural and normal that the questions which an historian puts to the past are those suggested to him by the events of his own time, and much can be learned from the pursuit of such inquiry. What is improper is when the concerns of his own time suggest not only the questions but also the answers. In almost every ex-colonial territory tremendous efforts were made to rewrite the past—first, to reveal the imperialists in all their well-concealed villainy, and, second, after that, to restore the true image of the pre-imperialist past which the imperi-

[22] On North Africa, see John Wansbrough, "The Decolonization of North African History," in *Journal of African History*, ix (1968), pp. 643-650; idem, "On Recomposing the Islamic History of North Africa," in *Journal of the Royal Asiatic Society*, 1969, pp. 161-170; David C. Gordon, *Self-Determination and History in the Third World*, passim.

alists themselves had defaced and hidden. It is at this point that the imaginary golden age once again makes its appearance. It is exceedingly difficult for even the most conscientious historians to be fair to former and fallen masters. Even now, fifty to a hundred years after the ending of Ottoman rule, the historians of the Balkan and still more of the Arab states have the greatest difficulty in doing even minimal justice to the Turks.[23] It will probably be a long time before historians in ex-colonial countries are prepared to discuss the achievements as well as the crimes of the great European imperial conquerors and proconsuls.

In the meantime, there is the more attractive and exciting task of rediscovering or inventing the golden age—the glories of medieval Islam, of Hindu India, even of the Barbary corsairs. In some parts the problem presents peculiar difficulties. Thus, for example, in much of tropical Africa, little is known of the history of these countries and peoples before the coming of the white man and of the written records which he produced. At one time, during the heyday of Kwami Nkrumah, a wholly spurious history was foisted on the black man in over-compensation for

[23] For Turkish views of the Arabs, see A. J. A. Mango, "Turkey and the Middle East," *Political Quarterly*, xxviii (1957), pp. 149-157. Cf. the works of Gharā'iba and Laroui, cited in note 9 above. For a Turkish study of Arab anti-Turkism, see Ilhan Arsel, *Arab milliyetçiliği ve Türkler*, Ankara (Ankara University Faculty of Laws), 1973.

his comparatively recent arrival on the stage of history. Black civilization was traced back to a remote antiquity and the exponents of this view sometimes went to absurd extremes. Thus one historian alleged that the ancient Egyptians were black and suggested that European Egyptologists had deliberately destroyed thousands of mummies to conceal the evidence of their blackness.[24] Another, rightfully inveighing against the wickedness of the Atlantic slave trade carried on by white men, was uncomfortable when reminded that the Arabs had been doing the same thing across the desert and the Indian Ocean for very much longer and argued that Tippu Tip, for example, one of the greatest and most notorious of the Muslim slave-traders, was in fact doing no more than "running a kind of domestic employment agency." Fortunately African historians rapidly evolved beyond this kind of thing—it took several centuries in Western Europe after the departure of the Romans—and are now more seriously engaged in recovering the earlier history of their countries by means of archaeology, anthropology, and straightforward historical research. But the recovered history of Africa is still painfully meager and the temptation to invent is often there.

The history of Africa raises another question—the invention not only of history, but of the very entity

[24] Cheikh Anta Diop, *Nations nègres et culture*, Paris (Editions Africaines), 1955, p. 20; cit. David C. Gordon, *Self-Determination*, p. 27, cf. p. 110.

whose history is written. Traditional historiography has usually been of chiefs, kings, or priests, of cities, countries, or empires—in other words, of the unit of identity, allegiance, and authority. The romantic age added the history of nations, in the romantic, subjective sense of the term; the age of critical scholarship added the history of institutions, of ideas, even of practices and of trends. Today, using an abstract formulation borrowed by historians from geographers, we also have the history of continents.

The ancient Greeks divided the inhabited world into two parts, which they called Europe and Asia, and then subdivided the second, making three in all. The third was called Libya. The Romans adopted the same classification, substituting the name of Africa for Libya. The boundary between Asia and Africa was sometimes placed on the isthmus of Suez, sometimes on the Nile. The same tripartite division was maintained by medieval European geographers, but is rarely mentioned by the makers or writers of history. Towards the end of the Middle Ages, the use of the term "Europe," as indicating a real entity with common aspirations, becomes rather more frequent.[25]

There are two points to note about this tripartite classification into continents. The first is that it was a purely European concept, from Greek up to mod-

[25] See Santo Mazzarino, *Fra Oriente e Occidente*, Florence (La Nuova Italia), 1947, pp. 41ff.; Denys Hay, *Europe, the Emergence of an Idea*, Edinburgh (Edinburgh Univ. Press), 1957; Federico Chabod, *Storia dell'idea d'Europa*, Bari (Laterza), 1967.

ern times, and was unknown to the indigenous peoples and cultures of the other two, who were unaware even of the names that the Greeks and Romans had assigned to them. The second, related to the first, is that, of the three, only Europe represented any kind of real historical entity, with a common culture derived from Greco-Roman and Judaeo-Christian roots, and a common sense of its own identity as against the rest of the world. In this sense, the idea of Europe is a continuation of Hellenismos, Latinitas, and Christendom.

In the vast continents which Europeans called Asia and Africa, there was not and could not be any comparable sense of identity. In the Muslim lands, geographers divided the world into a series of "climates" (*iqlīm*), cutting across the three continents, but the really significant division was between the House of Islam (*Dar al-Islām*) and the rest, the House of War (*Dar al-Ḥarb*). In the remoter lands beyond Islam, in China, India, and sub-Saharan Africa, the parochial preoccupations of Europe were entirely unknown. It was not until modern times that European influence, European power, and finally European scholarship persuaded the inhabitants of Asia and Africa that they were Asians and Africans, and that this fact had some political and historical significance. Yet even now, the division remains artificial and misleading. The conventional boundary between Europe and Africa is the Mediterranean—yet the Sahara is at least as effective a barrier, and the peoples of the North African littoral have far more in common with their neighbors in Southwest Asia and even with their neighbors in Southern Europe, than with the peoples south of the Sahara. This is substantial justification for President Senghor's identification of Africa with negritude. Similar or greater objections could be raised to the notion of Asia as an entity, stretching from the Eastern Mediterranean to Japan, with dubious boundaries in Turkey and the U.S.S.R. The writing of Asian and African history in our time furnishes many striking examples of the triumph of ideology over reality, of will over fact.

I return to my initial themes—to Cyrus and to Masada. The celebration of the Cyrus anniversary at Persepolis was criticized at the time by some foreign observers as a piece of costly and pointless display. It may well have been costly; it was certainly not pointless. On the contrary, it was a classical example of the skillful and purposive use of history. The splendid parade and ceremonies at the tomb of Cyrus and by the majestic ruins of Persepolis dramatized as never before one of the major processes in modern Persia, and one of the main aims of her rulers—the transformation of the Persians from a religious community to a secular nation, with the core of their identity, the form of their loyalty, no longer Islam but Iran. The process is underway, but is not yet completed, and some further help was felt to be necessary. The basic theme of the celebration was the millennial continuity of the land and people of Iran, through successive cultures and religions, and the role of the institution of monarchy in sustaining it.

Similarly, the cult of Masada in modern Israel is no doubt designed to restore the long-submerged political aspect of Jewish identity, together with its military associations. But the choice has its dangers. Cyrus, as has already been observed, marked a beginning, Masada an end. When the Jewish collective memory forgot Masada and instead chose as its symbol Rabbi Yohanan ben Zakkai escaping from Jerusalem and seeking the permission of the Roman conquerors to open a rabbinical seminary, it showed a sound instinct. Masada was a dead end in Jewish history. Beyond it lay nothing—oblivion. Painful as it may seem, it was the path of Ben Zakkai that represented realism, survival, and a future—that is to say, swallowing one's pride, seeking the good graces of the master of the land, and trying to preserve the Jewish heritage and identity through the faith and the law. Today Masada has been recovered, and indeed fully recovered, not merely in the pages of learned archaeological journals but firmly ensconced in the popular awareness of Jews and indeed of others, both in Israel and elsewhere. Care is needed not to carry it beyond the stage of recovery into that of illusion. Dedication and courage are both noble and necessary—but they must not lead again to self-destruction in a dead end of history.

Index

LIBRARY OF CONGRESS CATALOGING IN PUBLICATION DATA

Lewis, Bernard.
  History—remembered, recovered, invented.

  Originally presented as the Benjamin Gottesman
Lectures, Yeshiva University, 1974.
  Includes bibliographical references and index.
  1. Historiography—Addresses, essays, lectures.
2. History—Philosophy—Addresses, essays, lectures.
I. Title.
D13.L46 1975   907'.2   74-25607
ISBN 0-691-03547-4   9-2-75